To Mrs. Brunion
a lovely lady
a dedicated American
a generous spirit

Tom

(Psalm 121:1-2)

"Chrissie, I Never Had It So Bad..."

"Chrissie, I Never Had It So Bad..."

by Tom Haggai

THOMAS NELSON INC.
Nashville / Camden / New York

Copyright © 1973 by Thomas S. Haggai

All rights reserved under International and Pan-American Conventions. Published in Nashville, Tennessee by Thomas Nelson Inc. and simultaneously in Toronto, Canada by Thomas Nelson & Sons (Canada) Limited. Manufactured in the United States of America.

ISBN Number: 0–8407–5044–7

Library of Congress Card Catalog Number: 72–13901

Preface

On various occasions my speeches have been printed in periodicals; and often, after I have addressed a convention, the sponsors have asked that I allow them to have the address sent to the full membership. All of this I have found flattering. Now it rather frightens me to realize that these speeches are in book form, where I can't change a single word.

You see, I *never* read a speech. I prepare a full text—that's what you'll read in this book—but I try to talk *with* my audience, not *to* them. It has been said that my addresses are more "happenings" than speeches, because there is interaction between the audience and me.

Several years ago I changed my method of speaking. Until then, I always delivered what I had prepared, whether it was right for the audience or not. But I realized that my purpose in life was to minister to people and that requires that I say what a particular audience needs to hear. Now I prepare myself as thoroughly as I can, filling my head and heart and soul with all that God can inspire in me and through me; and that becomes my game plan. But I'm always ready to change it, to do whatever is necessary. You will also note that I stick with the simple rule that every speech should have three S's:

There should be a *Smile,* something that gives people a moment to relax. Of course, there usually is some humor before the address starts; but within the speech itself there also should be a Smile.

Second, I think every speech ought to make *Sense;* and by that I mean that it should appeal to the mind.

Third, I believe any speech should have *Soul;* it should appeal to the finest instincts of a person.

I always try to add a fourth S—a *Sob.* I try to get an emotional reaction to back up the Sense in the speech.

Actually, this book started to be just that—a book written from beginning to end. But I found the discipline of writing a book not only unfamiliar but also very time-consuming, and I didn't have the time to devote to it. After struggling for four years, I felt that what most of you would rather have would be a book in which you could read a speech of mine you had heard, or perhaps a speech your friends had told you about. That's how this book came to be. If reading it is in any way helpful to you, then I will feel that my ministry will have taken on an added dimension.

The speeches really do not belong to me; they belong to the audiences that have shared them with me, to the people who have encouraged me and shared my heartaches as well as my happiness.

To you, I give thanks. And for making the speeches readable, for getting down on paper what I try to communicate with voice and pauses and gestures, I express my profound appreciation for my right arm, E. L. Ludgin.

As I say on radio each day across the country, "May God Bless You."

—T. S. H.

Foreword

Having traveled millions of miles in a lifetime I have met and known tens of thousands of individuals, but none for whom I have a higher regard or deeper affection than Tom Haggai. In my estimation he is one of God's noblemen, and is endowed with unusual talents which he dedicates in glorious fashion for the benefit of Almighty God, our cherished Republic, and his fellowmen.

Certainly he is outstanding on America's platform circuit today. He has an unusual technique, and his audience rapport is such that the messages from his heart and mind and lips are enthusiastically accepted by those of every walk of life; by teenagers of the current generation and by those who make up the older establishment. He has a spirit which reaches the hearts of men and lifts them up. He does not take the middle of the road on any subject related to values but is ever ready to stand up and be counted. He gives his listeners terrific goals which can be achieved in playing well on the gridiron of life.

For years I have urged him to make permanent, between the covers of a book, some of the thoughts he has shared with his thousands of enthusiastic listeners so that they might have the opportunity to savor the full flavor of his thoughts. His philosophy is not only sound, but it is practical and workable in these troubled days of turmoil and chaos in the world scene as it involves mankind.

For those who have been privileged to be in audiences addressed by Dr. Haggai, this volume will bring forth vividly the "Dr. Tom" that they have known and heard.

For those who are daily listeners to his five minutes of inspiration on the "Values for Better Living" radio program, this book will crystalize the Haggai formula of life and living. And those who have never known or heard Tom Haggai will undoubtedly be richly blessed as they revel in his personality and in his delightful and effective role as a crusader for worthy living.

H. Roe Bartle

Contents

	Preface	5
	Foreword	7
I.	What Troubles Our Troubled Youth?	11
II.	"Chrissie, I Never Had It So Bad . . ."	43
III.	The Gray Beard Advises the New Beards	75
IV.	The Dream of a Perfect World	103
V.	The Spirit of '76	133

Prefix to Chapter I

WHAT TROUBLES OUR TROUBLED YOUTH?

Each of the chapters in this book is a speech, but when I deliver any of them, it doesn't come out the way you read it here. Each audience is different, and as I feel the differences, I change the speech. I make the same points, but sometimes in different order. I guess you could say that each audience collaborates with me in creating a speech. What you read in this book is the result of taping each speech and then rewriting it hoping it will make sense to you as a reader—as a part of a silent audience.

This first speech has been given before all types of audiences —many Chambers of Commerce, teachers' groups, even before the National Association of Manufacturers. I've been most pleased with the response. Men who are leaders in their communities have come up to say, "You've helped me relate to my own children." But many would add, "And what you said is going to help me in my sense of priorities about what we should do in this community." That really pleases me. They have things in the proper order. Sometimes people want to do everything for their community and not start inside their own homes. Audiences seem to get what I believe is a very important message; I hope you will, too.

I. What Troubles Our Troubled Youth?

Has there ever been a father who looked through the triple-thick glass of the maternity nursery, as a nurse held up the brand new, pink, wrinkled baby who would carry his name, and thought, "Sixteen years from now, my biggest problem will be understanding this child and having him understand me"?

No, fathers don't think like that. He'll look at this man-child and think of hopes and dreams . . .

His son as a star athlete in high school or college . . .

Little League baseball . . .

Learning to swim . . .

Cubs, Scouts, Explorers . . .

Baiting the first fishhook with his boy . . .

Hunting trips . . . maybe even Canada . . .

College . . . it doesn't matter which one (as long as it's *my* alma mater) . . .

A good job (with any company, so long as I approve) . . .

Marriage (to the girl he loves, who'll come from a *good* family). . . .

No father, looking at his son for the first time, anticipates any difficulties with him . . . but the biggest problem, sixteen years later, and maybe for a decade after that, will be simply *communicating* with his son. And that problem may stand in the way of the realization of all those dreams and hopes.

The historian Edward Gibbon has provided the favorite text for modern Jeremiahs who prophesy the death knell of the United States. Point by point, our history has been compared with the decline and fall of Rome, as explained by Gibbon. Although there is merit in the comparison, it is dangerous to limit it to the surface problems . . . for instance, that there was a steady decline in morality in Rome before her fall; therefore, the steady decline in morality in our society (as our Jeremiahs see it) means we are fast approaching our fall.

Below the surface, though, there is a common ingredient in the death of the classical Greek culture, the decay of Rome, and the decline of other, more contemporary powers. That common ingredient is the development in each of a dual society—two societies in each culture separated by age. The young and the old occupy the same world, but see it differently; they share only material things, not a common outlook.

Our major problem is not racial, economic, geographic or military; the problem we must solve, to remain a strong society, is to prevent ourselves from falling into the same trap —to keep ourselves from becoming a dual society divided by age.

When the ruling generation (almost always the elders, though today we may be approaching a reversal) becomes falsely secure, they let their communications with the other generation slip. Then innocent misunderstandings—blamed on the passage of time—become sources of mistrust on both sides.

The generation gap is not new; it should be neither surprising nor the cause of dismay. Differences and distances between the generations are to be valued, and guarded. If we did *not* have a generation gap, it would mean either that we had a bunch of little old men and women running around or that we were very childish parents.

But handling our generation gap, keeping it alive and vital, requires two things of us: seriousness and communication.

What Troubles Our Troubled Youth?

Think how amused we were with the original student protests; we were pleased to see our youth breaking down the pre-World War II walls of regimentation. We took it all lightly. Hindsight tells us rather unkindly we should have been busy communicating; but we had other things on our minds . . . we were busy, too busy, with *serious* things.

Have we learned our lesson yet? Early in 1971, President Nixon was interviewed by one representative each from the commercial networks and educational TV; the purpose was to give us a candid appraisal of his previous year in the presidency. If I checked my watch correctly, they spent one twentieth of the time dealing with the problems of youth, and most of this on the single tragedy at Kent State.

As boring as the war in Southeast Asia has become, as explosive as the Middle East remains, as uncertain as the business indicators are, no problem that faces either our President or our nation has the serious implications of the "youthquake." Somehow, it must demand a national priority higher than a registration-controlled conference at Estes Park; it requires more consideration than one twentieth of an hour or more of interview.

If you feel we are already too late, then tune me out now. Or if you are super sensitive to criticism, crawl into your shell, because you won't like what I have to say. I will not absolve youth of all responsibility by blaming us, their elders; but I will face the problem the young are trying to scream at us.

Digest all the gripes, the accusations and the criticism coming from our young; boil them all down and we come to one basic complaint:

> Since World War II, our youth feel
> they have been more exploited and
> used than raised and trained.

Hear the complaint again. It is an accusation of our generation, and we must file our answer.

> Our youth feel that they are being exploited and used—not raised and trained.

How do we plead—guilty or not guilty? Before I give you my answer, let's look at what we've been through. Usually, we don't learn from history because we feel it is our privilege to live it for ourselves; our youth don't learn from history because they don't know it!

We forget that the United States entered World War II suffering from a king-size inferiority complex. We were still reeling on the ropes, punched silly by the Depression. The rest of the world was, too, but we were only connected with the rest of the world with the sputtering, hissing and distant voice of short-wave radio; and we were too caught up in our own problems to care. We felt isolated in our misery. We had somehow frustrated the dreams of our founding fathers; our industrial genius had somehow fallen victim to a shattered stock market and as the market fell, so did our sense of national destiny.

We came out of World War II the No. 1 nation of the world—not because we had sought that lofty position but chiefly because not one bomb was dropped on us and because the forced draft of wartime production had made us build an incredibly strong industrial complex. After the war, we were so strong we could plan further growth for ourselves and at the same time continue aid to our allies and even help rebuild our enemies—the first such action in history!

No person can mature in half a dozen years; neither can a nation. We were still shaky from the Depression surgery; the war miracle tasted bittersweet and left us with a private shadow of guilt. We could not tell which was the real United

What Troubles Our Troubled Youth?

States—the one that suffered the Depression or the one that won the war. While we suffered with the problem of deciding, the rest of the world was proclaiming us No. 1—some in congratulation and heartfelt gratitude, some in envy, and some to butter us up in order to get some of our aid.

The G.I. coming home may have had his secret doubts, but he was intoxicated with his role in having made the United States the undisputed *Champion of the World*. With Hershey bars, K-rations, Camel cigarettes and the G.I. smile, he had crossed all language barriers and was hailed around the world as the "benevolent deliverer," not the "conquering oppressor"—even in the lands of our enemies.

With the shouts of acclamation still ringing in his ears, he stepped from the gangplank of the troopship to collect his pay; his efforts to save the world should now rightfully be rewarded. The reward he wanted most was status; through the G.I. Bill of Rights and its dozen variations and options, he was out to better himself in every way, but particularly economically. The paternalism and well-defined lines of pre-war society were out; so were the old rich. The new rich and those ambitious to be rich drew the new lines; the moderate pace of living of the 30's was replaced by the frenzy of the post-war "grab it while you can" race. If we were rich enough to feed the enemy, surely the ex-G.I. didn't have to be haunted by the empty feeling he remembered from the 30's.

Status became the goal; money was the means. A Chinese philosopher who died 300 years before Christ was born said: "To have enough is good luck; to have more than enough is harmful. This is true of all things, but especially of money." Chuang-Tzu couldn't have described any better the situation of the kids born after the war.

With the post-war years came the post-war baby boom. It was the earnest desire of the parents to protect their children from economic suffering of any kind—by earning enough, by being "involved" in enough of the "right" projects so the kids would grow up the right way. The child was to be an embellishment of his parents' image; the most glittering jewel on his mom's charm bracelet, the shiniest medal on his dad's proud chest. He was to have everything denied his Depression-born and war-weary parents—everything but love.

He was destined to grow up lonely, while his parents earned everything for him. Gradually at first, then more rapidly, our children realized something was missing. "Presents without presence" weren't enough. Material gifts weren't even appreciated; the child had never been without, so he didn't know how valuable they were. He felt bought, kept and smothered—and alone. Dad's successes left him unimpressed; and Dad's successes required more boards, more committees, more ego-feeders that kept him away from home even more. Mom's social climb left her too tired—and maybe too high—to "mother." Everything the parents did could be called good, and so recorded; the community shouted its praise. Only the cynic stood on the edge of the applauding crowd—the cynic who was their child.

He did the only thing he could. He made friends on the street to substitute for his ambitious but absent parents. He would stick with his own kind—the young. The dual society, so fatal in Greece and Rome, was beginning to form; the generation gap was widening.

So today we attempt to recover from the mistakes of yesterday and yester year. And parents of today are asking the right questions: "Do I want that which is best for my child, or do I want that which is best for *me* through my child?" "Am I interested in my child's improvement and development into a person in his own right, or is my child an extension of my own ego?" "Do I want my child to do what he can do best, or do I want to live vicariously, through him, getting belated satisfaction for my ambition through his achievements?"

Each parent should want the best for his child; but there is a fine line between wanting the best for the child and wanting to mold the child into our own image of what we might have been, what we wish we could have been, or (most dangerous of all) what we know we should have been. Each child is an individual—not the means of instant reincarnation for his parents.

Here is the father who takes his son into the den and talks about the shelfful of trophies (most of which Dad bought, unearned, to impress the girl who is now Mom). Dad wraps his arm around his son's shoulders and says, "Look what your dad did in school. Now you know I'm counting on you, son." Well, the boy happens to be bowlegged, knock-kneed, pigeon-toed and flatfooted, all at once; as an athlete, he's got nothing but problems. He starts off with a sense of impending failure; then he's inevitably frustrated; finally he's resentful.

In some areas of the country we are thinking of dropping Little League baseball. Not because it isn't a great sport; not because the kids can't take the game and learn much from it. No, the competitive lessons have been lost in the pressure from the parents in the stands on the coaches, the umpires, and especially on the kids themselves so Mom and Dad can say, "That's my boy!" A friend of mine couldn't eat for three days when his lad struck out three times in a crucial play-off game. There's religion for you—one day of fasting for each strike-out!

There are times when I feel it must be all right for a priest, rabbi, or minister to "doctor" the truth. Here he is, innocently visiting one of his parishioners, when Mother says, "Janie, play the latest song you've learned for our minister."

Well, it's tough enough when she's studying piano, but when it's the violin, it's impossible! They screech through, and at every screech you feel like cringing; and just as you screw up your face, you feel the eyes of the doting mother staring at you so you change the cringe into a grin; and it is physiologically impossible to cringe and grin simultaneously. And when the agony is finally over, the minister says, "That's fine." He *is* being honest; what he really means is, "That's fine—thank goodness it's over and I don't have to suffer through it any longer."

The mistakes on the piano, the screeches on the violin, are absolutely necessary as the child learns to play the instrument. The question here is, "What is the motivation of the parent in having the child learn to play at all? Is it a genuine desire to have the child learn to love music, or is it a way the parent can show the child off?"

It's not just a question of trying to get our children to produce in such a way that we can be proud of them rather than ashamed. There must also be the willingness to stand by them, in a time of mistakes, to give them the realization that a mistake doesn't finish life. We may be disappointed in their failures, as they are; but we cannot show our disappointment to the extent that we actually make them give up and quit trying!

How often I have had mothers come to me and say, "How could my daughter do that to me?" when their daughters were in trouble. I have had to say, "Mother, I know you are hurt; but my concern is not with your hurt right now. Rather, it is that here your daughter is coming into one of the most blessed moments of life with fear and trembling and anxiety. We must help her see that one mistake does not bring down the curtain on all future graciousness."

Or here's the father who says, "How could my son do that to me?" I say, "Dad, I'm sorry that your son flunked out of your alma mater, where you pre-enrolled him even before you knew your wife was expecting. But my concern is to help your son."

We must give our children the feeling that we are there with them. So often I have said to my children that I hope, for their own sakes, they don't break the rules of God and society, because there is always a payday some day; but I want them to know that, no matter what they do, they're mine. I'm their father, and I will stand by them.

Oh, it will hurt if they break into pieces; but if they do, they and I will get on our knees together to try to put the broken pieces back together. You see, I want them to come to me with their mistakes, as well as their joys. For I feel that, in the joys, any of us can laugh; but in the mistakes, we really learn to love each other.

Wasn't it my clansman, Kahlil Gibran, who said that we forget people with whom we laugh; we never forget the people with whom we weep? As much as it hurts, the weeping experiences parents have with children are what really ties them together.

If our children feel that their mistakes will always be thrown up at them, then they have to go outside the home to find solace and comfort. They feel they have been worth their weight in gold to the parents but thrown aside as soon as they are tarnished.

In the home with more than one child, there is another side to this. We must not allow children to compete with each other to the destruction of all. Each child has his own personality, his own capabilities and capacities, and his own goals to accomplish.

With my parents' permission, let me share this with you. I came along the third of three boys. Of course, that's an interesting role! Even now when I call home, my mother will say, "Is that you, John? Ted? Oh, you, Tom!" (I'm sure glad

I'm not one of seven—Mom might not be physically up to the roll call!)

When I went to school, if I studied hard I was "John" to the teachers because he made good grades. If I had a normal day, I was "Ted" because his grades weren't so good.

We went through school in a small town—four rooms and eight grades. John knew public relations, sat in the front row, looked up in the teacher's face. He had a quick mind, so he got straight A's. That's all you had to do in a small school. Some of us forget the difference between today's impersonal, consolidated school and yesterday's school. In the small town the teacher would face the parents walking to school in the morning, *and* at the post office and general store, *and* at the Grange Hall, *and* at the Volunteer Fire House. Now there's not a teacher brave enough to face parents that often and flunk their little darlings.

Ted came along, and he balanced the educational budget of our family. He was always the daredevil; there would be no challenge to making good grades but flunking would be something, so he always had a very interesting report card. He always had an A—one A in science. But all the rest lacked a great deal of being A's. In fact, many times they were P's.

Now you have to understand how they graded in that area of Massachusetts to understand P. They used A, B, C and then F; but just above F was P. What it meant was, "We ought to flunk you, son; but you are the son of the Baptist preacher. This is a Catholic community, and we don't want to be blamed with religious persecution, so we will just pass you on through." So, thanks to our Catholic friends, Ted was passed on through.

Well, Dad did everything to get those grades improved. He deprived Ted of privileges; he corrected him. That didn't work. My father is a firm believer in "taking the board of education and applying it to the seat of learning." He's a great psychologist as long as you're a great student; and if that fails, he gets to "the bottom of the trouble." But that still didn't produce a change.

Ted went on to Mars Hill College, North Carolina State University and graduate study in other places, and became a brilliant research engineer. You see, he had an unusual genius in science that made him bored with everything else. The law of compensation just meant that he couldn't be as sharp in everything else—or it would have been unfair.

He still has trouble writing a grammatical sentence; he really doesn't care whether Washington fought in the Civil War and Lincoln in the Revolutionary War or the other way around (and Washington doesn't care any more now that he doesn't even know what day he was born on). Ted doesn't care whether Columbus was a great discoverer or if he had an affair going with the Queen and the King chased him out of the country. But he had this unusual ability in science that could almost have been destroyed because of the most conscientious parents I know.

If there was that much pressure on Ted in pre-World War II days, think of what it must feel like to be young today. In our status-conscious society, we regiment our youth, resulting in sameness, tameness and lameness.

To give a child a balanced personality, it is imperative—absolutely imperative—that his parents look at him for his own worth. Not what they dreamed he might be . . . not what they planned for him before birth. He must be measured by his capacities alone, as they actually exist; he must be compared with himself.

We should share in his accomplishments and share in his disappointments. We are the first force that motivates him to be and become himself; we are the shoulder on which he should be able to cry. He *must* feel as important as any and every other child, particularly in his own family.

In earlier times, a child could gain something of the same sense of individuality because he was a part of a small community as well as a family. But in our time of hugeness, with eight out of ten of us living in cities, not villages, a sense of community is hard to find. Our children have to find it in the family, and with it, a sense of their uniqueness and importance.

Without a sense of belonging, the child feels the whole world is against him. He *must* belong . . . at least to his family. If his parents don't give him this sense of individual worth, of belonging, the result is a king-size complex.

At my first church, I looked out the door one day and saw one of our high school lads walking home when it was time for basketball practice. I hollered to him, "Red, not practicing today?"

"Aw," he said, "Preach" (and that's what he called me—just 'Preach'), "I quit the team."

I said, "Quit the team! Why did you do that, Red?"

"Aw, the coach picks on me."

Well, the coach and I were old athletic buffs together, so the next time I saw him, I asked what the story was with Red. He said, "Tom, that boy has more ability than my other four starters put together. He should get a college scholarship in basketball. I don't pick on him; there's just more there to develop, so I spend more time with him."

Red also said his teachers picked on him, so I went to talk with them. They said, "No, he's just a normal redhead. We expect him to be a little bit sharper, so we ask him questions more often." And I agree with their estimate, because when I was going to Furman and it came time for exams, I always jilted whichever girl I was going with and took up with a redhead. They always are just a little bit sharper . . . they have to be to compensate for their horrible tempers. (I can get by with writing this because Chrissie, my eldest, happens to be a strawberry blonde. She was born a redhead, is freckle-faced and, thank God, straightnosed—and this is a phenomenon, to say the least, in my clan.)

"Well," I thought, "I'm still missing the point with Red. Why does he feel everyone is down on him?" I knew his parents and his home life, but sometimes you need to go right into the living room to get your sense of proportion. Let me tell you about his parents. His father was going up; it was just a matter of time before he became president of a textile mill. But as he worked his way up, he was the right-hand man for the president. That meant the president would take on a job such as chairman of the United Fund and then come back to the office and say to Red's dad, "I took it knowing you would help me." Or perhaps it was the sustaining membership drive for Scouting: "I took it knowing you would help me." Or the Red Cross Blood Program: "I took it knowing you would help me." They were all worthy and honorable, and Red's dad didn't *have* to help—but he wanted to keep on going up.

So every time Red scheduled some project with his dad, the time would come and his father would say, "We're going to get to it; we're going to get to it. I've just got this one project to finish, and then we'll have some time."

Red's mother wanted to keep up with her husband; she didn't want to hold back his progress. So she was active in the book club, the garden club, the women's club; and she went all the right places, including the theater train to New York. And all the rest. And when she wasn't off at a meeting of some kind, she was usually afflicted with a disease called "bridge."

So Red has absolutely everything a boy could want. His shirts buttoned down on three sides (very "in" at that time), and he kicked off his shoes to put on his pants (before flared bottoms, remember?); he even had his own car. It didn't have three on the tree, but it had four in the floor. No hubcaps; they weren't "in" that season. You name it, he had it.

He had everything, in fact, but that which he needed most —a sense of belonging. When he arrived home at night, often there would be a note that said, "Eat all you want; it's in the oven staying warm for you. We'll be home after a while. Love."

Love. It's an easy word to say, even easier to write at the end of a note . . . but the word itself, without anything else, is meaningless. Red didn't even know where his parents were. I have found this true many, many times: I can find more teenagers at home at night who don't know where their parents are than parents at home who don't know where their teenagers are.

Now, everything Red's mother and father were doing outside the home was good. But they were so busy doing good and being part of the "do good" society that Red felt like the sixth wheel on a car . . . that he was really in the way, and if he were not there, his folks could be doing even more of their "do good" in the community. So, because he had no feeling of belonging, he felt the whole world was against him.

The former president of the American Management Association, Alexander B. Trowbridge, recently wrote on this very thing: "One of the most difficult and important questions facing the manager of today's complex organization is that of time, how to allocate it, how to use it to the fullest advantage, how to be sure that his time is devoted to things he, not someone else, should be doing." Mr. Trowbridge makes the point that so often the extra work a manager does means that his home is robbed because he gets home after the children are asleep . . . and the home is sacrificed to the job, rather than the other way around.

John Kemper, the headmaster of Andover, puts it this way

when he talks about the current mood of our young people: "I've often wondered if the post-World War II generation hasn't been one deeply preoccupied with its own affairs. It seems to me that we have been incredibly busy with our own careers and the avocational demands made upon us. The requirements of job and profession seem to increase and become more complex. The greater one's success, the more he is in demand to serve on community projects and on countless boards and committees of the multifarious institutions that do society's good works . . . educational, civic, social or cultural.

"It's not easy then to find the time and thought needed for the young. The interests we have we don't share with our boys and girls, with the result that they struggle to develop their own, which we don't share either. Hence, neither we nor they find the other very interesting. This I think is what the 'generation gap' really is."

Red rebelled because he felt left out. His dad ignored him, probably throwing up his hands once the rebellion started, saying, "Red's a real disappointment." That was the scene in the 1950's; son rebels, dad ignores.

The 1960's brought a new phenomenon: The youth became weary of the guilt that their rebellion created. They felt rejected by their parents so the rebellion was justified, but they were tired of being on the defensive. The youth of the 1960's would say, "To hell with your world where you only use me for your satisfaction. I'll create my own world." Some turned to transcendental meditation; some became "Jesus freaks"; and many, many turned to drugs.

Today we have again the mythic situation of Cronus who tries to devour his children as the children are thinking that if they castrate their fathers, they will be free. Red quit the team in the 50's; now youth "turn on" and join another team.

We do have a tendency to oversimplify, and I must refrain

from doing so. The reasons young people use drugs are many. In our surveys, however, both on the campus and with the military, the single most important reason—equalling all others put together—is that they feel unwanted in our world so they "cop-out" into a world of their own.

When they lose their sense of belonging in our world, they look for a world that will grant them full citizenship and welcome. And drugs do it. The common reaction to drugs, whether it be marijuana, heroin or LSD, is that the user feels immediately self-sufficient. He is now sitting on top of the world, looking down; he doesn't need you, me or anyone. As Roger Miller sang, he's "King of the Road" (and he tells us he was "on it" when he sang that song).

A young airman stationed in England told me, "The only real friends I have here are my fellow users." Freud believed that to preserve a healthy, sane mind, one has to avoid loneliness and to feel a certain self-respect. When the child moves from the feeling of being unwanted in the home to the regimentation of military life or to the impersonality of a large university, he is a prime prospect for a pusher. Psychiatrist Dr. Bruno Bettelheim has aptly called drugs "the instant" for young people—"the nurturing mother they never had." A former addict, now seventeen, agrees saying, "Drugs are a return to the womb; you feel warm, enclosed, safe."

A beautiful 19-year-old came into my office. She had a beautiful face and an equally beautiful "bod"; she had a lot going for her—and it all looked good when it was going! (As you can see, my clerical background didn't destroy my 20-20 vision; or just because I'm on a diet, that doesn't mean I can't check the menu!) As she sat before me in her mini-skirt testing my powers of concentration, she told this story:

"Last year, during my senior year at high school, most Fridays I took the 8:10 a.m. Eastern flight to Washington and

What Troubles Our Troubled Youth?

the 2:00 p.m. flight back. I brought with me enough for my habit—enough, that is, to supply my pushers in order to finance my habit." She waited for me to look shocked; when I didn't, she went on. "You know my daddy" (and I do—an executive with a local firm). "Call him, or call mother, if you can locate her at the club. Tell them my story. I'll give you documented proof of my actions, but neither one of them will believe you. Either they'll hang up on you" (and here is what haunts me), "or they'll just cuss you out. Mr. Haggai, I just wish either one of them loved me or knew me well enough to believe I can be bad . . . bad . . . bad!"

A schoolteacher called me from Tampa, Florida: "You don't know me but I listen to your radio show, 'Values For Better Living,' every day. At our junior high, we've had to dismiss about fifty boys with venereal disease. Finally, we traced the culprit. She turned out to be a 13-year-old girl, hooked on dope, who is selling herself at $2 a crack to afford the habit. Mr. Haggai, she comes from one of our finer middle-class homes."

When I started preaching, at age 12, in the slums of Boston, including Scollay Square, drugs were being used all around me. I couldn't excuse the users, but I could understand them. They were desperate for relief—any relief, no matter how artificial—from their rat-hole existence. But today, the rapid increase in drug use is not among the slum dwellers; it's among the suburbanites.

There is nothing new in what I have just told you; the figures have been in for years. But when we are confronted with alarming figures, instead of being glad for the alert, in our selfishness we look for excuses. We have been saying, "Yes, drug usage is increasing—but the rise is among the poor, the blacks, the ghetto people."

To succumb to flagrant self-deception like this only delays

any possible cure. Take it from me, and write it down in your heart, as well as your memory: the drug scene is part of today's culture.

I have been talking about the youth who are now users; but when I say that drugs are part of today's culture, I do not mean just the other side of the generation gap. We must keep in mind that the profit from drugs is made by syndicates of adults exploiting youth. As long as drugs are profitable, they will be promoted until their use becomes an acceptable habit for the "in" crowd of the "now" people.

Can I emphasize the point so we will not forget it? Our generation is making the profit. Our generation is bringing the stuff into the country. Our generation is trying to seduce youth into using it. The drugs are being painted as "beautiful," "grassy," the "end thing," "mind expanding," and even as "that which facilitates your relationship with God" Are the sellers succeeding? I'm afraid so.

My generation of non-users asks, "Why use drugs?" The young people to whom I speak ask, "Why not use drugs?"

Hopefully, at this point the thought of your son or daughter using any form of dope makes you break out in a cold sweat; it does me! But what can we do to prevent it?

Remember, the greatest single reason for use given by this generation is their feeling of rejection by our generation—not the only reason, to be sure, but the most important, the most common. Sure, some turn to dope out of curiosity, or for mind expansion, or from fear of the future, or boredom, or from sex problems; but none of these reasons, and not all of them put together, equals the number who say they use drugs because of the feeling of rejection, alienation and rebellion.

The means of correcting the problems are not unknown. A group of prominent behavioral scientists confirmed for me that what I have been saying, over and over, in speeches is simple but workable. We seldom fail because of what we

What Troubles Our Troubled Youth?

don't know but, rather, because we don't use what we already know.

Here are my four simple but positive suggestions:

I. Example

First, let me make it clear that I'm not using the term "example" as you might expect a minister to use it; I am not dealing in the realm of what we call "simple morals." True, it would be difficult for a father who drinks too much to argue convincingly with his son about drugs. Sure, there is a difference in the effects; the drinker usually drinks himself "out of it" while the drug user is often "turned on" in an effort to "get with it." But the causes are similar; both are using artificial means to avoid facing their problems.

The executive who comes home to suburbia and instantly fixes a drink feels he must drink to relax from the tension he has left over from his day. He can't resolve the tension-causing problems himself, and he can't face or accept his inability to resolve them; so he looks for artificial relief. And the real reason Pop or Mom puts bourbon on their cornflakes is to get enough artificial courage to face the day. The alcoholic escape artist differs very little from the teenage dope-user.

But when I use "example" as my first positive suggestion, it is in another light. I am told today's youth are the first generation born without optimism, and maybe I've found out why.

One of my cherished rewards in speaking all over America is not just meeting the respected gentlemen who have built and are building our country but also hearing from them how they succeeded. I love success stories—even embellished. Men with a spark in their eyes and excitement in their voices have told me how they started . . . with a mouthful of tacks and built a furniture empire; with half a dozen knitting machines and built a hosiery corporation; with a corner

"Mom and Pop" store and built a supermarket chain; with a janitor's broom, after school, and climbed to the presidency of a bank; with a box of tools and rose to own a new car agency; with a night clerk's job which led, eventually, to an executive job with a luxury hotel; as a sandwich vendor to later own a swank eating place; with a small grove of trees which grew to a packing plant . . . and on and on they go.

Talking with men like these in 1971 gave me a clue to the example we are giving our youth. What did they say? "President Nixon ruined it all!" I'm not defending the President; I'm illustrating how we glow with our accomplishments and how quick we are to find someone else to blame for our failures. We accept all the credit for our successes; someone else—a scapegoat—gets the blame for our failures.

Sure, business was bad the last of 1970 and most of 1971; as "Slappy" White, the black comedian, said: "Business was so bad even those who didn't intend to pay wouldn't buy."

But what kind of example are we giving when we take such a passive attitude toward difficulty as to merely look for someone else to blame it on? Little wonder our youth lack optimism when they find our pins are so easily knocked out from under us. They see we are happy to smite our chests in victory but too proud to bow our heads humbly in thankfulness.

And as we cannot accept either defeat or imperfection, they find evidence to support their feeling of rejection; we obviously don't need them when things are going well, and they're sure we'll "split" on them or blame them when they reveal weakness by coming for help.

If you feel I'm belaboring the point, think back to any normal conversation in your home about 6:00 p.m.—or better yet, tape one.

"What a day! Nobody wants to work any more!"

"I've got to have the slowest secretary in the office."

What Troubles Our Troubled Youth? 31

"How he ever became group vice president, I'll never know—he's thick!"

"They badgered me into buying stock and just look at the market!"

"Those foreign imports make competition unbelievable! Where are the true Americans who invest in America?" (This was said by the owner of a Toyota.)

Have you fathers ever heard yourselves saying things like that?

Or mothers, does this sound familiar?

"You think things are bad for you—you ought to try putting on the Bazaar with that bunch of social climbers on my committee."

"Our neighbors just have to be the most inconsiderate people we know."

"If the company really appreciated you, I wouldn't have to work."

"Don't give in! Push for what's due you—and us!"

"Why don't you fire him?"

"When I got married, I thought at least I'd have a new home. . . ."

Where is the thanksgiving? How much do we expect? Is cheerfulness only for the good times, to be forgotten when things are tough?

Little wonder youth think the whole living "scene" is all bad. Little wonder they have no hope.

Sure, we all have to blow off steam occasionally. But when have our young people heard us say, "Today was one of those challenging days that tapped my skills—and my patience! Really tough, but I guess I shouldn't complain. We have our home, and our family and more than we really need. God's been good to us."

Just as everybody is attracted to a joyous person—whether business is good or bad, whether everything pleases or not—

so youth are drawn to the parent who radiates hope for the future, thankfulness for the present, acceptance of the past. By example, we can be guiding lights for our youth.

II. Time

Of all people, you may well feel I should be the last to talk about giving time to the young . . . making sure they know they are important because they can command some of our time. But traveling as much as I do, I'm very conscious of the danger of neglect.

We are the only culture where the whole family doesn't enjoy even one meal together. The home used to be the site of industry, a place of piety, and the garden plot of democracy.

The fields, the barn or the wagon shed were the main source of income, and the rightful place for men and boys to work and earn. The henhouse, the barnyard, the spinning wheel and needle and thread by the fireplace and the kitchen were the centers of industry for women and girls.

The home was the sanctuary of worship; what was learned at home was reinforced at church and in Sunday School, not the other way around.

And family discussions were the prep schools of good citizenship.

Father was a prophet, a priest and a king. He taught the Word of God; he led the family in worship; he enforced moral law.

Today, Dad clasps Mom's hand and says, appreciatively, "You can thaw and heat up a meal as well as my mother ever did!"

What are our homes today? Well, let me see. They are dormitories by night, commissaries by day. Home is where you go to get ready to go somewhere else.

The living room is a sprint track between the bedroom

where we dress and the front porch where someone is picking us up.

When I would eat dinner with my late Uncle Joe, if I couldn't spend two hours eating, I wouldn't insult him by sitting down. You ate, chewed, swallowed, burped; ate, chewed, swallowed, burped; then you swallowed, burped, ate . . . until finally, having gotten filled, you could eat and burp simultaneously. But all the time we were eating, Uncle Joe was discussing business and family affairs with his boys. Discussing, too, not just lecturing . . . he listened some of the time at least. It was good therapy!

We've lost that kind of dining, and a great deal with it. The sharing groups, group dynamics, dialogue groups and all the rest are a good but still superficial substitute for the old-fashioned family affair. They indicate the hunger for sharing that those of us who enjoyed it in childhood still feel, but even more the hunger felt by those who have never had a real family. I believe in such groups; I'm a charter member of the oldest one in my city, but they are only a pale imitation of the real thing.

In Taiwan, I commented to my Chinese host about the family compound being completely walled in. He said, "You Americans are different from us. We put a wall around us to protect us from the outside. But we have no doors between us. You are naked before the outside world, but build walls between yourselves."

To break down those walls in my family, I've found I have to set a schedule with my children; I have to make appointments for them as I would for a client. In addition, of course, I spend some time with them at meals, on trips and so on; but if I don't set aside time specifically for them, we never get together. When we do, we don't always plan our conversation; it's free-wheeling. But the communication, the sharing, is the essence, more than the words.

No matter what we discuss, the time together draws us closer.

That is the positive side of spending time with your young people; there is also a chance to use time to prevent a negative. If they spent more time with their children, many parents could nip drug usage in the bud. Time to observe lets you become aware of:

> changes in habits
> lack of sleep or eating
> a down-trend in studying before it's reflected in lower grades
> new friends you don't know, or sloughing off old friends
> a new nervousness
> bloodshot eyes
> a newly acquired sloppiness and inattention
> misuse of money
> a needled arm.

Time, which has always been a healer, can also be a revealer.

III. Awards

Note that I am not suggesting "rewards" but "awards." There is a difference, and it's important. Rewards are based on the idea that if you do such-and-such, then I'll do such-and-such in return. In business, that's honesty; in the family, it can become either bribery or blackmail.

When I say "awards," I mean an expression of appreciation which you initiate. It could be as simple as saying, "Son, I'm proud of you—you've done a great job in school." Or it can be something tangible, like, "Son, we want to plan something special for you this summer because we're proud of what you've done in school." It could be, "Daughter, you've made us the proudest parents!"; or, "When you were a little girl, we designed your room for a little girl. Now you're a young lady, and a lovely one at that; so we want you to help us fix it up the way you'd really like it."

These are not rewards; they are awards . . . an expression of close observation, knowledge and gratitude for what a young person is and has done. They are not limited to your own children, or your own family; it might be that you would want to go down the block and say to a young man, "I'm the old codger who lives up the street from you. I just saw in the paper that you made Eagle Scout. I was a Scout myself; I never made Eagle, and I just want you to know that I'm proud of you."

With me, the greatest words I hear are from the people who come up to me after I've finished a speech and say, simply, "Thank you." In fact, I think I actually have to hear the words, "Thank you," every day of my life to survive and go on. Surprisingly enough, our young people are exactly the same.

Another way to give an award, not a reward, to a young person is to include him in a family council planning a summer trip, a vacation, or any other family event. I don't mean to suggest you let young people rule your life; but if you have done a good job of disciplining them, and if they understand their proper relationship with you, then they will not expect to have the final say. They will be flattered at being asked for their opinion. This not only confirms a positive self-image for them but it also automatically opens up communication with them.

So the third suggestion is "awards." Remember, an expression of appreciation for what a young person is or has done—not bribery or blackmail. Award, not reward. Or, to put it bluntly, when was the last time you looked a youth in the eye and said, "Thank you"?

IV. Believe They Can Be Good

Here I am not suggesting that you put on rose-colored glasses and adopt the attitude that your son or daughter can do no wrong. Just because we're human, we're liable to make mistakes; as I've pointed out, it's important for children to learn, from very early, that everybody makes mistakes some of the time.

But I believe that at times you and I talk so much about the faults and mistakes of our young people that they figure if they don't go out and do something wrong, they'll disappoint us; they think we *expect* them to go wrong.

Another all-too-human fault is that we tend to generalize too quickly, and to categorize, to pin labels on people or things, even quicker. And being impressed by headlines, we forget they are made by the exceptions; they are not the rule. When the headlines tell the tale of the young people who are rebellious, we read the tragedy of those few, forgetting that they are the exceptions—we generalize—and then we categorize by throwing our own young people into the same category.

And it's amazing how people live up to our expectations of them; when you firmly expect someone to dislike you, he feels your animosity and is more likely to dislike you. When you expect someone to succeed, and are counting on him, he is more likely to succeed.

To help our youth become all we hope and dream they will, we must believe that they can be good!

A couple of years ago Chrissie came to me and said, "Daddy, I'd like to go to Myrtle Beach for a weekend." That's a lovely beach in South Carolina, about 220 miles from home, and a Mecca for the young. Of course, she had planned this well in advance.

I asked, "When would you like to do this?"

"I'd like to leave either tomorrow evening or Saturday morning." This was Thursday evening—how do you like that for advanced planning?

"Chris, I think that's a good idea, because I've got to speak on the West Coast over the weekend; and then I'll be in Myrtle Beach to make an address on Monday."

Then she threw in the clincher: "Daddy, I'd like to *drive* to Myrtle Beach." She was 16 and hadn't been driving long—and never as far as 200 miles. To encourage me, she added, "Cindy will be going with me." That wasn't much help—one 16-year-old counseling another while driving 220 miles.

But again I thought, and again it was fine; she was a good driver. So I said, "Good. Chris, if you don't mind, I'll get in on Monday; and if you don't have any plans, we'll have dinner together. Then I'll ride back with you on Tuesday."

Of course, I never considered what it would do to me to ride 200 miles with a 16-year-old driver. It's actually a rather beautiful drive; but from my position on my knees in the back seat, I could hardly expect to see a thing!

When it was time to leave on Friday, I started through the routine of telling her what to do and what not to do, how to drive, where to go and all the rest. Then I pounded my head and said to myself, "Dumb-dumb! You are going to make exactly the same mistake you counsel other people all across America not to make! After all, you've done all that you can, for 16 years, to raise her to be a good girl. Anything you say in a last-minute lecture now isn't going to change a thing. In fact, she's so excited about leaving that she's not even listening well. You'll just have to count on having done a good job up to now."

So instead of a lecture I simply said, "Chrissie, would you mind sharing your plans with me?" And she did.

She told me where she would be staying—with one of my

favorite hotel owners, Milton Bauchner. Then she volunteered that she would check in with Mr. Bauchner each night so he might know when she was in her room. I found the rules she laid down for herself were much more stringent than the ones I would have given her. So she went; and as far as I know she had a good weekend and did not break any of her self-imposed rules—and we had a good time coming home together.

You see, it is difficult to do, but you and I *must* believe that they can be good. We must count on that, and we must realize that if we have had their attention for 15 or 16 years, then we've molded all that's going to be molded; we just have to have faith that we will not be disappointed in their behavior.

There are my four suggestions; and I can almost hear the intellectual saying, "Such simple suggestions! I just don't believe that in this complicated set of problems of dealing with young people they are sufficient."

Would you pardon me if I suggest that maybe one of our troubles is that we have become so intellectual and sophisticated in analyzing the problems of youth that we have wasted the opportunity of actually *doing* something. We have been so busy analyzing and re-analyzing, instead of doing something, that they are actually lost in the shuffle.

My four simple suggestions, if you want to open lines of communication with your or anybody else's young people so they can feel a companionship with you and you with them, can be wrapped up in these key words:

    I. Example
   II. Time
  III. Awards
  IV. Good

What Troubles Our Troubled Youth?

I'd like to close this chapter with a story. For 14 years, every pair of shoes I wore was provided by Gilbert Bernard. He built the business of his Gilbert's Shoe Store in High Point, not so much by the keenness of his mind and his ability to forecast what business was going to be, but by his untiring desire to satisfy his customers. Besides providing a wide range of shoes for lady customers, he ordered custom-made shoes for a few male friends, of whom I was privileged to be one.

About four years ago, a severe coronary forced Gilbert to sell his store and in March, he and his lovely wife, Marion, went to Florida for their winter vacation. Marion had to do all the driving; Gilbert wasn't strong enough to drive more than short distances.

On a rainy day in Fort Myers (it does rain sometimes in Florida), he stayed in the car while Marion did some grocery shopping. She came back to find he had not been able to take his eyes off a couple across the street. They were shoeless and had the intentionally ragged look some of the young people affect today, but Gilbert felt the young man looked sick. "Marion, that young man is in trouble; and I've got to see what the trouble is."

Marion told me later, "I wanted to tell him, Tom, 'If anybody has trouble, it's *you;* and the last thing you need is exposure in this weather.'" But she didn't say it, she knew it would do no good. Gilbert bounced out of the car, in the rain, and went over to find out what was going on.

The story? The young man had been told he had a lung problem, and they wanted to get back home to New Jersey so he could have an operation. The young lady said the only money they had between them was a $75 personal check her father had sent them, but no one was interested in cashing a personal check.

Well, my friend Gilbert took over; he was always ready to help his fellow man, especially if he were young. Gilbert did these foolish things: He put the couple in his car (risky because that meant he was liable for them). He took them to a nice but reasonably priced motel where he paid for their room; when the clerk was reluctant to register them because of their dress, he announced they were his son and daughter-in-law. And he told the couple his room number at the Holiday Inn in case they needed him.

All that night, Marion said, Gilbert tossed and turned, wondering what more he could do for the young couple, worrying if he had done everything possible. Next morning, in pouring rain, the couple dropped in. Gilbert dried them out, put them in his car, drove them to the bus station, purchased their tickets, and sent them on their way to New Jersey.

Marion told me that this crossed her mind: "Here's my husband, sick with a heart problem, getting up and stirring around, doing everything for this couple—complete strangers —just as he would for his own." But she knew he could not rest if the couple needed him, even if they were con artists.

The sequel? After a few more days in Fort Myers, Gilbert and Marion moved up to Daytona Beach to visit friends and finish their vacation. And what Marion feared most happened. Gilbert's exposure to the weather had weakened him and given him a slight cold. After a day of mild fishing from the dock, he came in overtired, and early the next morning he died.

A heart worn out from work, maybe, but certainly from helping others.

So frequently he would stop by my office to talk about the problems of our day, and especially about our young people. He had always had too many young people working in his store for the store to be as profitable as it should have been,

What Troubles Our Troubled Youth?

but he wanted to give them summer and after-school jobs. There was never a student at High Point College who had a problem that I couldn't call Gilbert and he would say, "Tom, what do you need? What can I do? How much? You take care of it, and I'll be happy to pay the bill."

Gilbert was unique. He was a member of the Chamber of Commerce, but he was never active in a civic club and never cared even to be in a leadership role in the Chamber. He was generous to his synagogue but never especially active in it. In fact, he introduced me to the best pork barbecue in High Point; I always felt I went along so he could ask me to bless the barbecue. I would say, "Lord, if you can bless under grace that which you cursed in the Law, then bless this piggy to Gilbert's stomach."

Though he didn't express it in a usual way, Gilbert Bernard had a concern.

He had a heart for young people. Somehow, he was able to see them differently than many of us do. He did not look at how they were dressed; he saw what they were worth. He didn't question who they were, what their pedigrees were; he saw them for what they were—young people with fire in their hearts and all their future before them.

I close this chapter with this story because I believe that if there is any chance for us to help our troubled youth, it will be when you and I see them not for their garb (if it bothers us we might, like Gilbert, realize that they are just protesting and reaching out for attention with it) but for their worth . . . their potential. And having seen them as people, with problems, we do something about what troubles them. I have only given simple suggestions as to what can be done; the real answer, of course, lies in our concern—yours and mine.

Prefix to Chapter II

CHRISSIE, I NEVER HAD IT SO BAD

Many people are telling today's teenagers, "When I was your age, I never had it so good." I don't agree, and you are about to read why.

I've always loved my eldest daughter, Chrissie, but it wasn't until she became a teenager and started to become an adult that I began to see her as a person. Now, whenever I talk to young people, as I do in this speech, I'm really talking to her.

I'm always thinking in pictures, and one comes vividly to mind now. Back in the 'Nineties, William Jennings Bryan came to a town in North Carolina, near my home, where he spoke to thousands of people. They jammed two city blocks to hear him. That was before the days of amplifiers; he made himself heard by speaking in front of a sounding board that bounced his rich voice so that those two blocks away could hear every word. When I give this or any speech to a youthful audience, I feel Chris and some of her friends standing behind me as my sounding board. When they can accept and believe what I'm saying, my voice is heard; if they can't buy it, I can't say it.

II: "Chrissie, I Never Had It So Bad..."

The one question I am asked most frequently is actually a statement disguised as a question. Parents say, "Tom, you *do* believe the youth revolution is just about over, don't you?" And they usually get "uptight" when I have to answer, "No, I think that probably the youth revolution is just beginning." In the well-worn but still working phrase, I think "we ain't seen nothin' yet."

The revolution no longer takes the quickly identified form of a demonstration on the streets; now it's disguised. It's being assimilated into the Establishment; our youth are no longer as concerned with confrontation as they are with working *within* the system to bring about their revolution.

A couple of years ago a sales manager who sat next to me during a banquet summed up the parents' puzzlement. He put it like this:

"Tom, do you remember reading recently that the students at Iowa State University elected the perfect personification of a hippie as president of the student body?

"My son and daughter are both students there, and we couldn't wait for them to come home for Sunday dinner after the election. Almost as soon as we sat down, I demanded of my daughter, 'Whatever possessed your fellow students to elect a character like that?' I was sure she had more sense, but I thought she'd be able to tell me what the other students, the ones who voted for a hippie, were thinking.

"She looked at me with her sparkling eyes and replied, 'Daddy, before you say any more about my fellow students,

I've got to tell you *I* voted for him, and if you check with your son you'll find that he voted for him also.'"

The father didn't tell me what his children's reasons were; whatever they were, he didn't understand them. And he said to me, simply, "Tom, why? What could attract my son and daughter to vote for someone who represented the very opposite of everything they were raised to believe in?"

We Americans are born optimists, and a bit conceited in our optimism. We are sure our young people really agree with us, deep down inside, and that any divergence from our beliefs they may show is only temporary. But as I said, I think the revolution the young people are involved in is only just started.

Let me hasten to remind you that "revolution" is neither good nor bad. We are a country born of revolution. It was a group of young revolutionaries at a bridge in Concord who fired "the shot heard 'round the world." It was another group of young revolutionaries who mixed the tea with salt water at Boston. But almost as soon as the Revolution began, we had a Declaration of Independence that put noble thoughts into noble words to explain to the world what we were about. And shortly after the war itself was over, our Constitution was adopted, formulating a revolutionary kind of government.

We revere these documents, often forgetting that they are the fruits of revolution.

Today, if we as adults have a role to play in the revolution our young people are engaged in, it is not to stop the revolution. That is an impossibility. Rather, we need to clear the lines of communication so we can join what experience has taught us with the zeal of youth. Only then can we give substance and meaning to this new revolution. We, the adults, must set limits so the wildfire burns only the dross while it refines the golden values of our republic.

To draw the lines, to set the limits so they are respected, there must be communication between the adults and the young. But before they will even listen to us, we have to get rid of some of *our* hang-ups:

1. We cannot "explain away" the unrest of youth today as a mere cycle of history. In general, our young people are responding to a specific set of conditions and attitudes that were formed while they were growing up among us. They are not against the Establishment because it is the thing to do, but because they feel unable to cope with it.

2. It doesn't help for a speaker to state, in a feeble attempt to pacify at college convocations, "You're the finest young people we've ever produced." All that does is turn them off; they read it as so much adult hypocrisy. They know you cannot judge history while it is still being written; their generation—and yours and mine—haven't been around long enough to be evaluated.

3. There is no comfort in the observation that "We have a *few* radical young people, but most of them are *great!*" A group of behavioral scientists meeting in New York recently disagreed on many aspects of the 'youth problem' but did agree on the following breakdown of the youth population:

7 per cent of our young people are radicals; of these, 3.5 per cent are extremely radical, belonging to groups like the Students for a Democratic Society (SDS), The Weatherman, and so on.

Thirty per cent of our young people are ours for the asking. They are active in their churches or synagogues, members of organizations such as the Boy Scouts of America, YMCA, YWCA, YMHA, Boys Clubs, 4-H, FFA and so on.

And 63 per cent are uncommitted . . . the silent majority of youth.

It seems that the 7 per cent who are radical have a greater

influence on the 63 per cent who are uncommitted than the 30 per cent who are involved do. My sales manager friend found that, though his son and daughter wouldn't join the radicals actively, they did in spirit. The reason may be that the radicals enlist a disproportionate number of the brightest, sharpest, most creative and talented youth, who are first admired and then followed by the masses. The bright ones turn radical because they see most clearly what's wrong around them, and are fired with zeal to correct things. We need their vision and their zeal, but, as I said, they need our experience to set limits.

Besides ridding ourselves of hang-ups, we can begin our bridging of the generation gap by honestly seeking to understand our young people. Bringing things into focus, seeing them clearly, opens our options to help. Let me try to clear our vision.

I. Knowledge Without Wisdom

I'm not playing with semantics. When I say knowledge, I mean the kind of information that can go very fluently from the textbook or the professor into the notebook of a pupil without passing through the head of either.

We have a tremendously knowledgeable group of young people. The high school graduate of the 1970's has been exposed to *three times* as much information as the high school graduate of 1950—and if you graduated before 1950, you're just plain out of it, Dad.

They have the whole world at their fingertips. They can go to any international airport in the United States and, in just 24 hours, be anywhere else in the world they choose. More and more of them are doing just that. And they're used to having wheels; thousands of them can migrate to Woodstock or to Florida for Easter without giving it a second thought.

They're used to seeing the whole world in their living

rooms. Television (and I liked it better when I stared at a round eye, not today's square eye) has so shrunk our globe that we, sitting in our homes, see distant events—elections, conventions, disasters, even wars—more clearly and know more about them than do some people in the rural areas of the countries involved. And beginning with Apollo 8, we all, but particularly the young, have seen that even the moon and Mars can be brought into our living rooms.

Their world is so small; at their age, ours was so huge. As I think back, I remember my grade school days in Massachusetts. When I made a trip with my folks from the little community of Holbrook to Boston, it was an event. When I went with my grandfather to see his pet Red Sox play ball, it made me something of a celebrity. And then in the summer when I went with my father to visit his relatives in Michigan, I came back as a local hero. My classmates wanted to know if, when I was way out West in Michigan—1,000 miles away from Holbrook—I saw any sign of Indians!

Today's young people know more about the capitals of the other nations of the world than my generation knew about the capitals of the other states of the Union.

Oh, they do have knowledge—they've collected all the information they need. I'm reminded of the mother who came to see me when I was still a pastor. She told me her daughter was asking interesting questions, and asked if I thought she should discuss "the facts of life" with her. My reply was, "By all means—because I think *you* are in for a liberal education."

Or of the father who thought it was time to talk with his two boys, Johnny who was 15 and Billy who was 13, and give them the boring bit about the birds and the bees—an exercise we fathers go through with our sons to help make the fathers feel better. Johnny caught on very quickly, but Billy seemed to be in a fog.

Dad said, "Johnny, sometimes Billy understands what you

say better than what I say. You know what I'm talking about; will you do me a favor and run through it with Billy?" And Dad heaved a sigh of relief as the boys went outside.

Johnny said, simply, "Billy, you understand about girls, boys, scoring, making love, making out, and all that stuff."

"Sure," Billy said.

"Well, Dad wanted me to assure you that the birds and bees do it in exactly the same way."

The 'facts of life' aren't all they know. In a more serious vein, George W. Beadle, a Nobel Prize winner in genetics and a former president of the University of Chicago, tells about one reaction to a speech he gave before a distinguished medical society. One of the doctors commented to his son, an undergraduate at the University of Chicago, "Dr. Beadle lost me in the first five minutes."

His son said, "Dad, that wasn't a bad lecture—but I learned everything he talked about in high school!"

I'm sure they have the facts about all kinds of things; in fact, I'm sure they have knowledge—a thorough grasp of the facts about all kinds of things. But knowledge doesn't necessarily mean wisdom, and I'm just as sure that they do not yet possess wisdom.

By wisdom, I mean not just the knowledge of the whys as well as the whats, and I mean more than just the knowledge of when to use which facts or formulas. By wisdom, I mean the ability to utilize knowledge to accomplish some endeavor which, hopefully, will be useful. I mean the ability to make knowledge practical. I mean seeing the value of knowledge—and here is where one of our principal troubles lies. We have, with unsurpassed education and information-processing networks, stuffed the young full of knowledge while raising them in a society so protective that we haven't let them acquire experience.

We've given them what Dr. Roy Meninger calls "our dedication to infantilize them." By extending the period of their education, we've kept them from the world of experience longer than any previous generation; we've kept them infants for nearly a third of their 'three score years and ten' by the time they graduate from college and take their places in the adult world.

What has made us so protective?

Is it because *we* are insecure, and we take out our insecurity on them?

Historically, we know that the purpose of a home—like the nesting of a mother bird—is to prepare the children for that moment when they are pushed out of the nest to survive on their own. We have delayed that moment, and the delay is part of the problem.

Over-protectiveness does not mean that we are better parents than the generations before us. It simply means that we are afraid to turn the young loose—which is really an indictment of us. We are admitting that we are afraid we didn't raise them properly.

For instance, I am one of the last generation that was allowed to walk to school. Now, mothers are nothing more than glamorous (glamorous?) cab drivers, carting their children to and from school. And on occasion, when I take my children at 8:00 a.m., I have the feeling that the sight of some of these frowzled, curlered, un-made-up moms could set the cause of womanhood back a hundred years!

You also know that the worst crime a teacher can commit is to keep a child after school, because this messes up the whole carpool arrangement both for the child's mother and the entire neighborhood.

And the children who are not taken to school by their mothers are generally bussed, often under a very illogical system.

Now think of it! I would have missed two-thirds of my

education if I had not been allowed to walk to school. What I learned in the classroom was minor, compared to what the upper classmen taught me walking back and forth to school; they gave me my 'earthy' education!

If my premise, that our overprotectiveness is a result of our own insecurity, is correct, then what has brought about our insecurity?

Maybe one reason is Hiroshima. Maybe, since the dropping of that one bomb, we have had to live with the fact that there are a dozen different persons in the world who have the ability to push a button and wipe a city off the face of the earth.

Maybe it has dawned on us that we have been worshipping the creation too much and the Creator not enough.

I think these are reasons, but I think there is another that is more important. That reason is that we are the products of a Puritan background.

I don't want to seem to be putting this down, because I think it is a wonderful background. But with its insistence on hard work and thrift and the other virtues of the Puritans, we have also inherited the belief that life on this earth is supposed to be a life of suffering.

Part of the Puritan 'hangover', as somebody has called it, leads us to feel that to be righteous, we shouldn't enjoy living. Suffering is necessary here because "we'll all have pie in the sky bye and bye."

I've felt this sense of guilt. Well do I remember calling my father some time ago and saying, "Dad, I used to think if I ever enjoyed living as much as I do now in my present work, it would have to be a sin. And if that is so, you are talking to the world's biggest sinner."

But I also think we all feel a sense of guilt about our affluent society because of this Puritan background. Most of us have more creature comforts than we ever dreamed we would possess. At the same time, we feel somehow we do not deserve the good life we have. Thus, we feel a little guilty.

Incidentally, I think this is one of the reasons we give so indiscriminately to so many 'good causes' in our country—not because we believe *that* much in helping other people, but because we feel some guilt about how much we possess, and it makes us feel better to give a little.

More importantly, because we feel this guilt, we feel that at any moment what we haven't deserved to have will disappear; at any moment, we may wake up and the beautiful dream will turn into a nightmare.

Have you ever noticed that we are constantly talking in good times about the depression—and more often than not it's from fear rather than from logic.

Almost every night of the week, I am speaking to the business community. Often, I listen to groups of older businessmen, standing around talking. They are not usually talking about the good business they are enjoying; usually the conversation goes something like this: "It hasn't been bad the first nine months, but, oh, I'm afraid of the last quarter. I'm just afraid that at any moment the bottom is going to drop out—and it may start in the last quarter of this year."

Now this kind of talk isn't because these men are keen students of economics. They're suffering from the Puritan hangover.

We simply cannot comprehend—or accept—our affluent society. And with this feeling, it's natural and normal for us to become overprotective of our children. We actually want to keep them from growing up—and we keep them from turning their knowledge into wisdom.

Our insecurity has become their restraint.

Pam, the daughter of two of my dearest friends, came to her debutante year and during the summer, she had a siege of depression. Her dad called me. "Tom, Pam is fond of you, and you seem to be able to communicate with her. If you have a moment, would you just chat with her?"

So I did, at the first opportunity. I asked what was bothering her, in what I felt should be one of the most wonderful summers of her life. I'll never forget her reply.

"Tom, it seems as if all everyone wants to talk about is, 'When's the next dance?'; '*What* will I wear?'; 'Where are the parties going to be leading up to the ball?'; 'Who's going to escort whom?' With all the problems of this world, it seems to me I should be doing something besides dancing my summer away."

Bless her! Pam was raised in a home that taught her a real concern for people, and she had learned well. She was raised at a time in history when she could see a world-wide need for this concern, and it seemed to her to be completely wrong *not* to be involved, somehow, in the human needs of the world.

She is not alone. Hers is not an abnormal reaction—it is normal! So many of our young people, brought up in our homogenized suburbs, sealed off from death and disease, the ugly, the crippled, the poor, feel they should do something to correct the deficient pseudo-communities they find about them.

Pam, like her contemporaries, was born with the Korean War. The Cold War was already three years old, at least. The Iron Curtain was christened before Pam was. A 'police action' suddenly came to mean more than the routine arrest of a lawbreaker . . . and would never mean less than war again. These, and other words freighted with horror, were household terms learned before Pam could read.

Perhaps most frightening, Pam had grown up in the shadow of the mushroom-shaped cloud. She had known all her life that a nuclear holocaust could happen. She knew that governments, like men, can err—but an error, now, means an-

"Chrissie, I Never Had It So Bad . . ."

nihilation. We, her elders, knew that wars were bloody and horrible, but never before were the preamble to total destruction . . . but Pam grew up knowing this.

Our young people want to be involved, and we need to get them involved. They are more than willing; we do not need to recruit them. What we have been doing is *keeping them from being involved*.

The young want to be part of the 'gut' of the society. We might well take the knowledge we have so generously shared with them and help them direct it into some helpful endeavor which, in turn, would help them attain wisdom.

How? We have to begin by examining our own thinking about young people and, if necessary, correcting some of our previous mistakes.

I was addressing a banquet for a group of churches in Virginia Beach one time, where they were concerned about having a 'constructive' youth program over the Easter holidays. (As you know Easter is a time when our beaches are sometimes torn asunder.) It has come to be the time of year when the college youth knock the Establishment after wiring home for the money necessary to afford the privilege. At any rate, the people who organized the 'constructive' program outlined it for me and asked, "Now, what do you think of what we've planned for our young people?"

I said, "It will fail!"

They were shocked. If I thought it was going to fail, why would I even come to the banquet?

"I *want* it to work, but it won't. Think about what you just asked me. You asked me about this program you have for the young people. It will only work when you begin to talk about the program you are going to do *with* the young people."

I don't want you to think I mean that our young people are to be responsible for *all* the decisions. No, I believe they will show respect for the generation before them, and share the responsibility for decisions. But they—and I—are weary of people constantly saying, "We have done this and this and this for young people, and they still don't respond." Young people want to have something done *with* them. They want to be *with* the action—not just be the recipients of whatever is given them by a benevolent society that has sought, all their lives, to overindulge them.

It is as simple as this: If you stuff a body with water— a constant inflow without any outflow—then you will either have a Dead Sea or a flood. Will you forgive this conservative if I should sound a bit liberal and suggest that I would prefer to see our young people flooding with revolutionary ideas —and trying to turn their knowledge into wisdom—rather than see them receive all the knowledge we can pump into them and then be satisfied to go to sleep and become like the Dead Sea.

From their desire to be involved, to turn their knowledge into wisdom, I can see hope and help for mankind in our generation.

II. Energy Without Direction

Wow! do they have energy! The quickest way to remind ourselves of how much they have to spend is to listen to their music. It takes energy even to listen to it without moving! And think of how they dance to it!

We did dance in the same way, though, didn't we? All of us who went through school with any kind of athletic scholarship, danced with all the same steps they use today. We started at the end of August or in early September, and we called it *calisthenics*. But instead of a combo providing the beat, we had a stuffy old coach barking out orders. And you know about old coaches: They never die . . . they just smell that way!

As I remind parents about dancing, I have to think of my own youth. I was raised by a father who is a very dedicated

Baptist preacher and who might be called strait-laced. That wouldn't offend him; he'd take it as a compliment. He didn't want me to dance while I was growing up, so I knew when I would sneak off to a dance that I would be in trouble when I got home. And let me tell you that when I finally did sneak off, nobody ever caught me standing six feet away, just wiggling, like today's young people! If I couldn't get in on a bit of the 'feel' and some of the 'action,' it wouldn't be worth the punishment that was sure to follow.

Seriously, young people do have energy without direction. I am tired of hearing people say that young people are lazy. They are *not* lazy. It's just that their energy is not channeled. When I was growing up, my energy was. All generations before mine, or almost all, had their energies channeled. By necessity.

To illustrate my point, let me tell you about something I told my daughter, Chrissie.

Being gone as much as I am, doing over 300 major speeches a year, I make a special effort to be home on my children's birthdays. When Chrissie was 15, I remember sitting down and just staring at her, knowing I should say something profound on her birthday.

At times, I've almost idolized her—especially after she reached her teens. Babies don't turn me on; I can buy a stuffed doll that will talk, cry and wet. But as a teenager, Chrissie became someone who could take issue, discuss, and enlighten me. She told me once, during her teens, "Dad, I guess you've always loved me . . . but now you like me." She was right.

So I sat admiring her, and finally I said this:

"Chrissie, when I was your age, I never had it so bad."

She opened both ears and began to listen as well as hear; she was used to adults who started preaching at the young with the opposite of that statement.

"That's right—I never had it so bad as you do. From the

time I was 12, I've been more or less on my own, economically. And that made life simple. If I wanted something, I went to work.

"You've heard my generation call this dedication to work morality; it was actually a simple, animal interest in survival. I like living better than the alternative; although I'm ready to go, I'm not homesick.

"Chrissie, if I were to go out into a field and corner an animal, hem him in, he'd fight to break loose. To survive. That was all I was doing. Delivering papers, picking strawberries, hoeing tomatoes, digging potatoes, mowing grass, shoveling snow, cleaning the church, sweeping college dormitory rooms—all the thousand and one jobs I did were the result of being cornered, hemmed in by the economic facts of life. I was fighting to survive!

"My generation has a tendency to glamorize those depression years; we make heroes and heroines out of depression children. But life was never simpler, or more serene. Every day we got up, fought to survive, and went to bed.

"We knew exactly what we had to do. College meant selling everything—including bike and chemistry set if you were lucky enough to own one. It meant using the ability to catch a baseball, to milk cows . . . all for the chance for education.

"Honey, my decisions were already made for me. My world said that if I wanted, I could have—if I put forth the effort.

"But you live in a different world.

"Whether you work or not, you'll be fed. Whether you work or not, you'll be clothed. Whether you work or not, you'll have the privilege of attending college. Yours is a world of options, not necessities—and life gets complicated by the number of options one has.

"If you walk into a restaurant and there's only one thing on the menu, you don't have any trouble saying, "That's what I want.' But when there are twelve choices, and you like

"Chrissie, I Never Had It So Bad..."

all of them, then you have trouble deciding. And if you're like most people, as soon as you give your order and somebody orders something else, you immediately wish you'd ordered that.

"Life becomes complicated in direct proportion to the number of choices you have to make. You're the option generation; I'm the depression generation. We tend to exaggerate the difficulties of those depression years, that lasted halfway through World War II—but that was the simplest life we ever lived. When I was your age, Dad never had it so bad as you do.

"So may you have the stamina, the values, the sense of what's really important, and the faith, to have a 'Happy Birthday.'"

What I said to Chrissie then I believe even more now. My children live in a world I never experienced growing up. The pressures on them—the questions they have to answer about what is right and what is wrong and why—are far greater than our problems of simple survival. By junior high school, their social life is equal to mine when I was a freshman in college.

Dr. Billy Graham said it better. Talking of his classmates and himself, Billy once said, "We didn't have time to sit around, grow a beard and wonder what our purpose was. We had to work!" I'm afraid his audience misunderstood him; they thought he was condemning today's youth. Actually, he was commiserating with them. He meant it was easier in his day . . . simpler. I agree. In the simplicity of our lives, protected and isolated as we were, we never had it so bad as today's youth.

So our young face the problems of being the 'option generation'; throw in the problems they face as a result of the post-World War II practice of 'permissive psychology,' and you have a king-size headache.

In its crudest form, permissive psychology can be defined as 'demand feeding.' When a child cries, feed him. If he has a temper tantrum, compliment him on expressing himself.

We blame our adoption of permissive psychology on Dr. Benjamin Spock. Dr. Spock has enough problems without our adding any more; and the only reason he is famous enough to blame is that you bought his books to help raise your children. Those books, once displayed on the coffee table, are hidden away now because of disagreement with Dr. Spock's political views. You hide the book under your side of the bed and it evens the lumps—Dr. Spock under your side, PLAYBOY under your husband's.

Dr. Spock didn't invent permissive psychology, and he didn't force us to adopt it; I think it is really one of the hells of war. World War II starts and Daddy goes to fight. Baby's born a few months later. When Dad comes home, he must be careful not to appear as an intruder; he doesn't feel he can step right in and serve as the disciplinary agent. Absence has displaced him from his position of authority.

We just got the family put back together and here comes Korea. The family again packs up to stay at Grandmother's while Daddy goes to defend democracy. Then the Berlin Blockade call-up. Then Vietnam. For three decades we've kept Dad away from the home. And no matter what Women's Lib says, with Dad gone, so goes discipline.

We try to explain Dad's war service, and justify it, by constantly telling the child it's necessary for Dad to be gone so a free world can be his. We make the world sound like the child's toy, rather than the child's place of service.

In our permissive society, the child is to be given something when he cries. Unfortunately, the child has far more capacity for crying than even our affluent society has capacity for providing. And when he becomes an adult, the child suddenly learns, rudely, that the world isn't his. At best, he is a steward.

"Chrissie, I Never Had It So Bad..."

But all his life crying has worked; and now, his cry becomes the whine of the wounded.

Even the young person who does accept responsibility while he is in high school has a problem. If he does want to work, many times he finds he simply cannot—because of the child labor laws.

These laws were developed in a period when child abuse had to be curbed; but that period has passed. Now, the laws need to be revamped so there is some way for children under 16 to work.

There is a further problem for the young person who wants to work—the minimum wage law. Say someone wants a summer job. An employer may want to hire him. But his 'entry jobs'—the jobs beginners must start with—are hardly worth the minimum wage the employer is already paying the people who will stay with him after the summer is over. The employer would be happy to hire young people at, say, $1.25; but if he has to start every employee—even temporary, summer help—at the minimum wage, it's then a different matter. He can hardly justify the cost to his stockholders or even to his own conscience.

It is not fair to expect any employer to become a minimum wage babysitter for three summer months for a young person who can hardly be expected to learn enough in that short time to contribute something back to the company.

Still, we must act—despite the legal hindrances. Last summer, while I was having lunch with a textile executive, he asked what I thought would be the most effective way to invest several thousand dollars to benefit youth. My answer: "Go hire several high school lads to work in your mill during summer vacation. Don't just hire them and pat yourself on the back for being a good guy," I added. "Each week, you or one of your top officials should take a coffee break or lunch with each of them, individually. Listen to what they have to say about your company, and to their attitudes toward business in general. Even if your company wasn't looking for a way to make a contribution to youth, I'd make the same recommendations. It is sure and certain cultivation for future recruiting."

We need to cultivate better relationships between many of our young people and the business community, but that is not the heart of the matter. And it is not important whether young people need jobs to survive, economically. They must have jobs to live *usefully*. The sense of accomplishment from doing a job gives them motivation and pride—and integrity. Most of them have money in their pockets already, but it has been given to them, and they rebel against being the wards of their parents, or of anybody else.

Without a job opportunity, the teenagers feel that their only work is school—a single, rather narrow-focused task. So they have either school or play; our society tells them they have no significant contribution to make. We are telling the person under 16 that he is immature, irresponsible and inexperienced—a real drag in our affairs. At best, he can enjoy only token participation with adults in the adult world, and he must remain in this state, no matter how mature he actually is, until he reaches the arbitrary but magic age we have agreed on for adulthood.

We show no respect for teenagers' individual talents, idealism, or enthusiasm. Except for school, there is very little he can do that is legal while he is under 16. We've made everything taboo. He can't work; he can't quit school; he can't vote; he can't enlist; he can't drive. When he turns sixteen, we let him drive, but that's all.

We withhold from the teenager both our virtues and our vices. There he is on the sidelines, bursting with energy, champing at the bit, eaten up with creative curiosity—and we deny him any possibility of participation. There he is with a pocketful of money, an educated drugstore cowboy, with nothing worthwhile to do! Is it any wonder, then, that so many turn to defiance, or rebellion, or worse, become dropouts?

Yet the legal age of responsibility has moved up, during the life of our country, from 16 years of age to 18 and now generally 21 although in some states it is being reversed. The reasons may have been good; the results haven't always been good. Think of it! During the Revolution, he might have been head of his home at 16; at 15, he might have been serving with the Drum and Bugle Corps in the Civil War.

A study by Frank R. Donovan, *Wild Kids,* reminds us that boys once entered Boston's Latin School, equivalent to high school, at age eight and went on to college at 14. Admiral Farragut went to sea as a midshipman at nine, and commanded his first ship at 20. Today, he wouldn't graduate from Annapolis until he was 22 or 23. In our past the young also acted, as Eric Hoffer says, ". . . effectively as members of political parties, creators of business enterprises, advocates of new philosophical doctrines and leaders of armies."

Thank goodness our youth are spared some of these burdens today. But just as overburdening causes breakdowns, so underburdening weakens, to later uselessness!

As an example of what I'm talking about, let me give you my opinion of *The Graduate.* You couldn't read the book or see the movie without forming an opinion. Maybe mine is different; it focuses on the collegian.

The problem of *The Graduate,* as I saw it, was having grown up with the thought that the world was there to serve him. He graduated from college with honors and was ready for graduate school when it suddenly dawned on him that the world he thought was to serve him was not acting like an obedient servant. He became rattled, and tried different avenues of escape—and found nothing but dead ends.

The world he had been told would serve him was about to crush him. And all his frustration was due to his having been taught to get, rather than to give. He had done the only thing expected of him—he had graduated. In the past, everything had been given him; how could he have learned to give? How could he have learned to accept responsibility?

"But," you ask, "how was it different in our day? How were we taught, in those dark and distant days of *our* youth, to have a different feeling about the world?"

It came to us subconsciously. Can you remember when you entered the first grade? The first preparation was to visit the family doctor, to be vaccinated. You *do* remember the old family doctor, don't you? He was the one who came to see you while you were still sick!

And do you remember vaccination? One of the nicest improvements in medicine is today's simple prick in the arm. In our day the doctor used a needle that looked big enough to scare horses; and he didn't just stick your arm, he went right through! I thought my rib cage would have a scar as big as the one on my arm!

Of course, you were warned not to knock the scab off or your arm would wither; so you knocked it off yourself (knowing the street bully would do it himself the first time he saw you) . . . and then all that night you stayed awake, checking the amount of wither.

After the vaccination, just as the doctor was unsticking a sucker from the bunch that stuck together in the humid April showers—the sucker was out-and-out bribery to get you to stop crying—he rubbed your head and said, "Now Tommy, you're going to be going to school. What are you going to be when you grow up?"

Of course, I had an answer: I was going to study medicine and hope I was the resident doctor at the old people's home where he ended up, because then *I* could give *him* a shot.

All kidding aside, like you, my intentions of what to be

when I 'grew up' ran the gamut—I wanted to be a policeman, a fireman, a bus driver, a doctor, a lawyer, a pilot . . . "a butcher, a baker, a candlestick maker . . ."

When Grandfather visited, he asked the same question in his own way: "What are you going to do after playing baseball?" He had been a professional ball player in his youth, and dreamed of the same for me. Auntie asked the same thing; everybody did. They all knew we would change a hundred times, but that wasn't what was important; we were being taught, subconsciously, as we started school, that we were to study for a purpose. We were to prepare to do. There is no free lunch.

Today, our tendency is to tell the child, "Have a great 'learning experience,'" (whatever that is) "and find your purpose later."

Our Orthodox Jewish friends could give us better direction. Not accepting Jesus as the Messiah, they are still looking for him. And when a Jewish mother gives birth to a son, she looks down with glowing pride that, to me, is absolutely beautiful. Actually, the glow is mixed with fear and dedication, because she looks at her son as the possible Messiah, the Deliverer of Israel. Whatever the reasons, she dedicates herself to oblivion and willingly becomes nothing to give her son a sense of commitment, dedication and purpose.

Again I expect an interruption. You ask, "Isn't it tragic to put so much pressure on our young people to choose their direction so early in life?" Pressure to perform actually gives security! And you ask again, "Don't people make enough mistakes as it is, when they have longer to choose? Aren't enough people finding they chose the wrong line of work or profession?" Granted, this could happen, but I suggest it happens as much—or more—with today's non-directional approach as it did in our generation.

Individuals often change their direction in life, but I believe no one should consider his former work a mistake so much as preparation for whatever he's going to do next. It is my firm conviction that it is better for a boat to be going downstream the wrong way, with a good rudder, than to be caught in the stream without any rudder.

Socrates à la Haggai: "For a man without a port, no wind blows well."

A sign on a building in Clayton, Georgia, reads: "You probably shouldn't be here, but aren't you having a good time?"

In Canada, especially, you still find colleges that require freshmen to state their occupational goal on their admission applications. Of course, the student is given latitude for change; but they believe he will do his best work when he has specific goals.

Another problem we have given our young people in college: Keeping the student cloistered on his campus separates him from the community, and contributes to making the college an island surrounded by the city rather than a vital part of it. And both student and community suffer from the separation.

As you can see, I believe we have wronged our young people by denying them the opportunity to make a meaningful contribution to society—other than going to school; by denying them a 'work ethic' and giving them, instead, a prolonged infancy from which we expect them to emerge, suddenly, as adults; and by not expecting them to take charge of their lives from an early age. No wonder they have energy without direction!

But that's not all. I contend that this energy without direction also contributes to the distorted attiude toward service to country which surfaces from time to time among the young.

Our young people *have* lost a sense of the usefulness of history; it is in vogue, and not only among them, to debunk our national heroes . . . the Lincolns, Jacksons, Jeffersons and Washingtons.

Because of man's innate need to worship, maybe we did give our heroes unquestioned sainthood; but we knew all the time that, being men, they had clay feet. The debunking of their character bothers me because it becomes a means to the end of devaluing history.

The purpose of the study of history is not to make anyone a slave to the past. At the very least, it can give us a sense of our debt to those who created what we enjoy. It can give much, much more. History teaches us we owe something to our country.

We think our young people refuse service to their country because they consider our foreign policy wrong or the war immoral. How academic sounding! I believe a major reason for the refusal of service of any kind to our country is a numbness to that sense of debt that history teaches.

Remember, we are raising 'takers', not 'givers'; and to them, service is a foreign word. 'Doing your own thing' *alone,* by yourself, is a denial of community; it creates an isolationism that makes impossible either united states or The United States.

With the sense of direction which only history can give, 'doing your own thing' will become doing something for your country; without it . . . well, it has been said before: "Those who do not learn from history are condemned to repeat it."

Let me take a last look at this from another angle. At present, we are discussing whether or not we are adequately teaching black history in our schools. Some feel that such teaching only encourages the concept of 'black power' and hence, racial separation. My feeling is that one of the best moves we could make to bring about social unity would be the teaching of *authentic* black history.

We whites need to know more about the blacks. More

important, when the blacks realize what their people went through in this country, and what they have contributed; when they (and we all) realize that the Supreme Court decisions were not brought about by contemporary pseudo-social workers, but that progress has been the result of their forebearers' sweat, tears, agony and almost infinite patience ... then they will choose to continue the orderly progress rather than be incited by the rabble-rousers.

I am strongly suggesting that when our energetic young people are given direction they see the opportunity, the obligation, and the commitment that are necessary for progress—indeed, for survival.

III. Courage Without Convictions

Actually, that heading should read, "They have courage without *our* convictions." And here is a basic reason why I temper my criticism of youth. I give them credit for their convictions, but recognize that they differ from ours.

If their convictions are different from mine, it means one of two things. Either I'm a poor salesman, for I've had a whole generation of time while they were growing up, to sell them. Or it can mean that my convictions could not stand the test of years.

Admittedly, the young people do a better job of protesting their disagreement with our convictions than they do expressing what they believe.

Vivid in my mind is a young airman in Aviano, Italy. During the question-and-answer period after one of my Commander's Call addresses, he became very critical of the United States. He said, "We, the United States, are not the best country in the world; we should learn from the other nations."

"You said two things," I replied. "I agree that we should learn from other nations. But if we are not the best country in the world, what are the better countries? Are we Number 3? or 5? or 9?"

He had no answer.

He could not come up with suggestions to help us, only criticism of our failings. He knew what he did not like, but he could not articulate what he wanted to replace it. That's the dilemma in which many of our youth find themselves, and they do not like their plight.

Where do convictions come from? Convictions begin when a child sees consistent behavior in his parents, and learns a consistent attitude and reaction to a given situation. Convictions are based on observed consistency.

But never do our youth—nor should they—accept our convictions carte blanche. Maturity is evident when they ask, "Do I believe what I believe because *I believe it* or because my parents say it is so?" When this happens, it is not a put-down of parents, but a discovery of self—and it can be a painful discovery. Doubts set in as the youth cuts his moorings from the parental harbor and sets out on his own beliefs. John Bunyan felt very much a 'pilgrim', but even he was sometimes imprisoned in 'Doubter's Castle.' Finally, light dawns when one begins to doubt his doubts.

But the reason a youth feels the strength—and the need—to leave the harbor is his foundation of faith, based on his observation of our consistency. And this makes the harbor a safe place to return to in a storm.

If convictions and consistency have this close a relationship, does this not almost answer the problem?

We are communicating with young people who grew up in a society where the President of the United States, who had been believed to be moral and upright by virtue of his office alone, openly and defiantly lied to the world about a spy plane shot down over enemy territory.

Of course, this was not the first lie openly told by a President, and then proved a lie; but now the news media turn spotlights into corners that previously usually remained dark, and then throw the result onto our TV screens for the view of the whole world.

You can argue the diplomatic reason; so can I. All I am doing is asking you to imagine the reaction in our children when we suggest, no, say positively, that there is a proper place for a lie. It has diplomatic immunity! At the same time we claim we can't have really close relationships with the communist world because they use 'the big lie'! Does that suggest that we know how to lie morally, while the Communists lie immorally?

Are we naive enough to believe our lies are used to help people, while the Communists use lies to injure people?

Take another problem: We know that for the nuclear world to survive, there must be peaceful coexistence. We are honest enough to admit we want to coexist because we could not survive a war; in fact, no one can win in the next world war. But we have to upgrade the image of the enemy so our people will accept coexistence. Thus we shield our eyes from seeing the crime of the 1968 massacre in Czechoslovakia; we portray China as a nation with a friendly team of ping-pong players.

Why do we have to whitewash the Soviet Union to accept coexistence with them? Coexistence is not for their sakes alone; it is for all of our hides, and all who live on earth. To make Russia appear good so coexistence is palatable to our people only clouds the moral overtones of our behavior, in the eyes of our youth. Coexistence and morality are not synonymous. Coexistence is necessitated by a nuclear warhead, not because either Russia or China is getting better . . .

or even more American. There can, and should, be honor among enemies for pragmatic reasons.

Let's take another look at Vietnam. We have tried—and failed—to sell our youth that the cause of our involvement in Vietnam was the defense of a helpless people. The defense of the right of a people to freely choose their ultimate destiny sounds heroic to many of us, but it's 'bunk' to our young. Let's admit a genuine purpose for our being in Vietnam is self-interest—enlightened self-interest. If we accept the 'domino' theory, fighting in Vietnam is protecting marginal real estate to protect ourselves.

In 1969 I was surprised to see more than 12 hotels under construction in Singapore. They felt they could well become the great international city of the 'third world'; they also were feeling the hope of a boom from the lucrative new oil finds in Indonesia, Korea and . . . Vietnam. Could it be we feel it necessary to have a hand in the development of this oil and trade? We are not wrong for having such interests, but let's admit them. Self-interest can even be admirable—but not when it's covered over with pious platitudes about generosity.

How can I sum up? What can I say to parents who, like my friend the sales manager, find they haven't communicated their values to their children? What can I prescribe as genuine medicine, not just a tonic, to cure some of the diseases of the spirit of our youth we have been talking about? A simple answer:

Honesty corrects the communication gap.

No matter who's on the opposite sides of the gap—be it the 'generation gap', the 'credibility gap', communication across the Iron Curtain or the Bamboo Curtain—the gap that exists is a communications gap, and the prime requirement for bridging it is honesty.

A few years ago a famed British minister spent the summer in my city of High Point on a minister exchange. At the end of his stay, I asked his impressions of our country and people.

His comments were complimentary, but when he analyzed the American church, he said, "You have a problem. You are hung up on black and white. To you, it's either right or wrong. That's how you *state* your convictions, but you *live* in the gray world. So, to youth especially, I would think you endanger credibility."

Try this incident on for size:

Several years ago, just before we really entered the jet age, I was leaving Birmingham, Alabama, on a DC-7 flight to Atlanta. Of course, in the South everything is funneled through Atlanta. As I have often said, I had my childhood arguments with some of my Catholic friends about purgatory, only to find it was just a question of semantics, because when you die, you are going either to Heaven or to Hell—but if you live in the South, you are going by way of Atlanta!

This was to be about an hour flight, arriving at Atlanta at 7:00 p.m.—when the Atlanta airport is one of the busiest in the country. But about half way there, one outboard engine on the DC-7 quit. The fellow next to me became extremely nervous. "What are you going to do? What are you going to do?" he kept asking. I told him I was going to sleep, if he would let me; but I saw that this wasn't satisfactory—and a few more minutes of his nervousness would make a mess of him and me both. Frankly, I must admit I wasn't too concerned about him right then, but I had to speak that night in the clothes I was wearing.

I had to say something, so I said, "You know, up in the cockpit we have one of this airline's most experienced captains." (I really didn't know who was flying . . . we might have been hearing a recording saying, "This is your Captain," for all I knew.) "He knows that this plane, especially with this load, is just as safe with three engines as with four. Usually when we get to Atlanta at this time we have to circle for another 20 to 30 minutes—almost half the time it takes to get there—before we get to land. But by shutting down one engine, he gets emergency clearance and so we'll land right away."

Well, this seemed to calm my companion, and when we got off the plane he said, "Reverend, I sure am glad I sat next to you. If you hadn't explained it to me, I think I would have had a heart attack."

Well, I had deliberately lied to him, just as I have been asked by doctors to lie to patients with terminal illnesses when the doctor felt the patient was unable to take the truth.

What is the answer? Are there degrees to lying? To morality? Are there shades of difference between truth and falsehood? I'll let you argue about that. What I will support is, "tell it like it is."

It is one thing to tell a lie—and quite another to lie about the lie. I know our President can't run foreign policy from a public platform. But tell us that! Tell us that there are secret negotiations or secret strategy. Don't tell us what's happening, just that it's going on, so we won't feel deceived. That's what keeps credibility gaps from opening between the President and the people.

A generation of youth raised on 'put-ons' tends to overreact. And with good reason. No one likes to have his intelligence slighted; no one likes to be made to play the fool. Now we have the world's greatest tools of mass communication; let's put them to good use. When we're "making one thing very clear," let's be sure we do.

Young people can understand and accept our weaknesses. They can't—and obviously won't—accept our arrogance about our frailties.

Our frailties can serve as a challenge to our youth to improve, to do better than we have done. My eldest daughter was in the audience when I said that the one thing I hoped she would always be able to say is that her father was not a hypocrite. Afterwards, I asked her if my statement was presumptuous. "Daddy," Chrissie said, "I am thankful that you have shared your problems and your anxieties with me, and encouraged me to learn from your weaknesses."

If I believe enough to call a belief conviction, I will not disavow even if I bend—or break. At the same time, I will not lie about my weakness. Instead, my children will see me struggle to pick myself up. My desire is not to be a pal to them, but a parent . . . neither perfect nor claiming to be.

Communication has brought about a different relationship between parent and youth. There is just as much respect as there used to be; idealism is just a little tarnished.

Conviction will result from their seeing the *real* us, and from their finding consistency in our behavior.

What can we say about youth? that they are

KNOWLEDGEABLE, BUT LACKING WISDOM

ENERGETIC, BUT LACKING DIRECTION

COURAGEOUS, BUT LACKING CONSISTENCY

We can't change our young people against their wishes, but we can keep ourselves from frustrating their fondest hopes.

And now, the test. Are you and I secure enough in our convictions about young people to turn them loose so they can add wisdom to their knowledge through experience?

Do we trust what they will do?

Do we have enough discipline to give direction to the energy of our youth?

Am I willing to live, in a believable manner, what I myself actually believe?

When did I last take inventory of my convictions?

It's a simple test to give, a hard one to take. The right answers might help all the "Chrissies" have a better life.

Prefix to Chapter III

THE GRAY BEARD ADVISES THE NEW BEARDS

This speech started to grow in my mind when young people began getting into small groups . . . the "touch" groups, the encounter groups. It was obvious that they were trying to find something to hang onto, something to really believe in. It occurred to me that the sentences that are the backbone of this speech, sentences from the Apostle Paul, have been giving people strength, something to hang onto, for nineteen hundred years.

I must admit I wasn't just trying to give them something to hang to. I was giving them a reason to believe that there is so much worth in each of them, that we would be the poorer if we didn't get to share it. Then, in order for them to be able to share, they had to be at peace with themselves. Otherwise their turmoil would keep them from sharing. Finally, I had to answer the question, "Why do I believe Paul? Why do I put any credence in what he said?"

While I no longer have a church in which to preach every Sunday morning, and a congregation as a captive audience, you've got to remember that I'm still a minister of the Gospel. Only now, speaking to audiences of many faiths or no faith at all, the answers to those questions are very important to me; and I try to get my audiences to see why.

III. The Gray Beard Advises the New Beards

Early in 1971 I was on the West Coast for the prayer breakfast of a national business convention; and whenever I'm on the Coast, I try to visit one of the colleges or universities in the area, just to rap with the students and find out what they're saying. That way I know what our students back East will be saying next year!

San Diego State gives you about as good an insight into the student culture as any institution you might choose; since I was in San Diego, that's where I went. I must say I was surprised and a little pleased when I discovered what the book was that most students were carrying. It seemed that everybody had one, whether it was hardback or paperback; some of the "fellows" were even carrying theirs in their purses! What was this overwhelmingly popular book? *The Sayings of Jesus Christ.*

I'm sure you've seen, or at least heard of, earlier books in the same series; it began with *The Writings of Chairman Mao,* the little red book carried and consulted by everyone in China, wherein Mao Tse-Tung provided maxims that, correctly applied, gave the answer to any problem.

Recognizing a good thing when they saw it, publishers in this country gave us the writings of Gandhi, the sayings of President Kennedy and of Sir Winston Churchill—even, after the Democratic convention of 1968, *The Wisdom of Chairman Daley* of Chicago, where there were such riots and protests against the Establishment. And now, *The Sayings of Jesus Christ.*

If I were intelligent enough or had enough business acumen, I'd like to publish the next book in this series myself, to get in on the profits as well as the royalties. I'd like to see a book of the writings of that marvelous intellect of Israel, Paul the Apostle.

Of course, they've already been published; they're part of the New Testament; and I'm amazed every time I read any of the many letters Paul wrote, because it seems almost that they were written fresh this morning, talking about the problems of today.

In fact, there aren't many of the writings of Paul I'd want to exclude; but there are a handful I won't wait to publish the book to bring to your attention.

The first is a phrase you young people used up until about a year and a half ago; now that you've dropped it, my generation is beginning to use it. (Maybe it was dropped when we began to use it, *because* we began to use it; I'll touch on that thought later.) Up until then, if your father was bearing down on you pretty hard about something you wanted to do or somewhere you wanted to go, your defense was usually a shrug of the shoulders and the statement, "After all, Dad, I'm just doing my own thing."

Or if you felt your mother was a bit too critical of one of your friends, you'd chastise her by saying, "Mother, everybody is entitled to do his own thing."

Believe it or not, the Apostle Paul used this phrase almost 2,000 years ago. He wrote this to his friends in Rome in the 12th division of that letter, in the second paragraph, according to the Phillips translation: "Do not let the world around you squeeze you into its mold."

Isn't that exactly what you mean when you say, "Let me do my own thing"?

Doing your own thing isn't just an excuse for having your own kind of fun; it's a responsibility for the way you live your life. Let me explain what I mean this way.

The Gray Beard Advises the New Beards

Every year I adopt a motto which I write in the flyleaf of my diary or my notebook. The motto I chose for 1971 went like this: "I do not want to spend my time this year doing that which everyone else can do, when I can do something no one else can do."

If that sounds like the statement of an egotist, read it again after you've read this. I'm not suggesting I have an answer for the world's problems that everyone is just panting for; rather, that motto reminds me of the responsibility I have to make my life as individual and distinctive as my creation.

One of the marvels of God's creation is that He never repeats Himself; He doesn't make duplicates.

Everyone knows that if you take a handful of snowflakes and photograph them before they melt and study them, they will all be six-sided and perfectly symmetrical; but each would be different from all the others. But consider this: There is no number in our language large enough to name the number of snowflakes that are trapped in the snowcaps at either end of our earth and on the mountain tops and in the glaciers; and even if you could name that number, it would have to be multiplied by another almost unimaginably large number of years since the first snowflake fell out of the sky for you to know how many snowflakes there have been since time began . . . and every snowflake that ever existed is different from every other that ever existed.

God is still more lavish in His creation of living things. Every leaf on every tree shares its shape with every other but has its own individual tracery of veins, its own face; every twig that breaks beneath your foot has its own character. And among men . . . well, the Talmud says it well: "If every man leaned the same way, the world would tip over."

You are an individual; there has never been anyone like you (and there must have been many times when your parents said, "Thank goodness for that"); you are distinctively made.

Even the two sides of your body are not the same. Your left hand is different from your right; the hearing of your left ear varies from that of your right; the vision of your left eye from that of your right; even the two halves of your brain, though they may seem identical in structure, have different functions. You gals, when you go to buy a pair of shoes, will try on a pair and find the left shoe is comfortable but the right one feels miserable. You keep on trying pair after pair until you finally get one that hurts *both* feet—and that is the pair you buy on the spot!

You are an individual; as a commercial for one of the leading insurance companies puts it, "There is no one exactly like you in the whole human race." That fact imposes on you the responsibility to *be yourself*.

I realize that one of your pet desires is that you do not want your generation to be a carbon copy of my generation. My plea to you is that you not try to be carbon copies of each other!

I don't think there is any danger you will be a carbon of my generation; I think there is great danger in the sameness with each other that you seek so strenuously. In fact, I think the emphasis you place on individuality is really another kind of protest, and like the other forms of protest you are prey to, it is a cover-up. You *say* you want to do your own thing, but your own thing is whatever everybody else is doing. This may well be a subconscious evaluation and appraisal of ours as an age of regimentation.

Daniel Boone said he moved whenever another family lived where he could see the smoke from their chimney; he needed room to be himself. We don't have that kind of room any longer, and with about 85 per cent of our population living in less than 5 per cent of our land, our cities are at

The Gray Beard Advises the New Beards

the point of explosion. We live so close together, we must learn new ways to protect the privacy of ourselves and the others around us, and we must insist that everybody conforms to the new ways. The regimentation that results seems to carry over into our other areas of living; it results in a sameness, a tameness and a lameness.

One of your reactions is that I never find you by yourselves; you move in "gangs" and "packs." And when you talk about individuality, you're talking about the individuality of one group of people, not of the people who make up the group —your group as opposed to that group, not you as an individual within a group.

It's tempting to give yourself up to the group; it seems to have so much more strength as a whole than any of its members, or even all of them acting as individuals. And it's tempting to react to other people simply on the basis of the group (or groups) they belong to; as soon as you find out what someone is, you know how to deal with him, how to think about him, even how to feel about him.

But each of these is a way of denying our God-given individuality—when you surrender yourself to a group, or when you react to someone on the basis of the group he belongs to.

We need, today more than ever, young people who are able to be involved with the needs and the projects of the day—involved with groups—yet who are able to retain their own identities within the groups.

Some time ago, speaking to a high school commencement, as I was going toward the auditorium I passed a girl who had purple hair. Literally. It also looked as though it had been styled by Phyllis Diller's hairdresser (before Phyllis had her remodeling job, that is)—with an eggbeater. I was fascinated; I don't believe more than one out of a thousand people is born with purple hair. She caught me staring and said, "You're looking at me because I'm different!"

I said, "No, honey, I'm looking at you because I saw seven other girls with the same weirdo hairdo." But I continued, "Why don't you give *yourself* a chance, and try doing your own thing?"

Way back in 1939—that's in the prehistoric era for most of you, I'm afraid—David Seabury wrote a book titled, *The Art of Selfishness;* it's been revised and updated a couple of times since, so maybe you'll listen to its premise: It's only when you're doing that which you enjoy most and that which develops your potential best that you are doing that in which you'll render the greatest service to the world and to yourself.

When you enjoy doing many things, it's tough to know what you most enjoy doing; it's tougher yet, when you're young, to know that which best develops your potential. And I'm afraid that we, in our Judeo-Christian tradition, have made things even tougher. We have taken some great Biblical concepts, such as that you must lose yourself to find yourself, and some wonderful Biblical words, like "consecration", "commitment", and "surrender"; and we have so interpreted these concepts and words to you that it seems they mean the more you dislike, or hate, or disavow yourself, the better chance you have of being right with God. They are hard concepts and words to put into practice, but they are not that hard to understand; and the meaning I have just given, that you have to hate yourself in order to be what God intends, is exactly the wrong one.

Not for a moment am I suggesting that you become a blatant egotist, but I must remind you that the only rule of sociology Jesus gave us is that you are to love your neighbor as yourself. Usually, we use that rule in relation to the second half of it—how you treat your neighbor; but if you don't have any appreciation of yourself, then your neighbor will have a heap of trouble!

In my counseling, I find the biggest problem I have is to

get a person to accept himself as he is, warts and all, sins and all. Somehow, we can forgive everybody else easier than ourselves; I can forgive you almost anything easier than I can look in a mirror and forgive myself the same sin. But it's only when I can accept myself that I can really accept you; I cannot love my neighbor as myself unless I love myself. And love, in this sense, means total acceptance of the good with the bad, the bad with the good.

Without this love, without this total acceptance of self, we are angry at ourselves for not being perfect; we can accept the fact that "Nobody's perfect" without interfering at all with our desire to be perfect ourselves. Whenever I find people who are angry, I am likely to find they're not angry at anybody as much as at themselves; the "somebody" they *tell* me they're angry with is a scapegoat for the anger at themselves they have no other way of expressing.

In our studies of the revolution going on in our country, we find that those who burn buildings, throw rocks through storefronts or slash tires and overturn cars are not really angry with the person who owns the property; they are actually uptight, frustrated, and angry with themselves, and they act out their anger by taking it out on somebody else.

Though I consider myself an ultra-conservative economically, I'm also considered a social liberal—though the labels, themselves, have their own built-in limitations. But after I've listened to all the advice of everyone about how to bring us together as a nation, I go back and think: If there's hope that we will be brought together, the secret is not my attitude toward you but rather, it is my attitude toward myself.

If I'm angry with myself and find I'm unacceptable to myself, I'll find a way to project my anger and disappointment with myself onto someone else; if I am at peace with myself, I can be at peace with you.

Walking into an auditorium filled with people, old or

young, I immediately have a warmth, an affection for them, and they feel it. This happens particularly with the young—because I accept myself, I respect you.

Let me repeat: Our anger with each other, which fuels so many of our social problems, is a reflection of our anger at ourselves.

A few years ago I made a trip overseas with Bob Brown, the marvelous individual who is a Special Advisor to President Nixon and considered to be the top black official in our government—a government which now has more black people involved than ever before.

Bob and I went to a beautiful retreat center at Berchtesgaden, Germany; there had been some misunderstandings, particularly between the races, and we went to see if we could help. You can't really say we were "white" and "black", for I guess I'd be considered somewhere in between . . . but basically white. We met with young men who'd come from bases all over Europe, mostly from places where there had been racial trouble; they were mad, yet they'd come to have dialogue about a problem that concerned us all.

I tried to put words into their minds. I said, "Now you white boys are sitting there saying, 'Isn't it wonderful—Tom Haggai is a friend of Bob Brown, a black man.' You black boys are sitting there saying, 'Isn't it wonderful—Bob Brown, a black man, is a friend of Tom Haggai, a white man. Maybe you think we're friends *because* he's black and I'm white; but that's not it. And I don't think I'll ever learn either to play tennis or to act well enough so we can get "I Spy" back on the air. No, we're not here to play the Bobbsey Twins in living black and white, the token biracial brothers. He and I are both here because the President, your Commander-in-Chief, and your Commanding General recognize that there are racial problems, and Bob and I both know something about racial problems. We're friends because I happen to like

Bob. I'm not so insecure about my whiteness that his blackness is a threat to me; he isn't so afraid of his blackness that my whiteness puts any fear into him.

"Let me tell you a story about how I learned about racial prejudice. From the time I was just a few months old until I was five, I was raised in beautiful Greene County, in the southwestern corner of Pennsylvania. When I was about four and a half, my father had to take Mother into little Washington, Pennsylvania, to see the doctor, and my middle brother, Ted, and I rode along. While Dad and Mom were in the doctor's office, Ted and I stayed in the car, looking at all the people.

"Well, down the street came a lady, and for the first time in my life I saw someone whose skin was darker than mine. I turned to Ted who, being five and a half, was the source of all my wisdom, and asked (using a word I've never used since except to tell this story), 'Is that what you call a nigger?'

"The car windows were down, and she heard me. The lady stopped, came over to the car, and slapped me on the face— as she should have. Then she said, 'Son, don't ever use that word again!'

"I bawled, more out of surprise and shock than hurt. And when my father came back, I thought that if I put on a real crying spell he would take up for me; so I pinched myself —hard—and cried.

"Well, when Dad finally got the whole story out of me, do you know what he did? He whacked me on the other side! And let me tell you . . . you've never been hit until you get a backhand from a Lebanese father; when you come back, you know you've been away!

"Then he talked to me, and through my tears I listened, and I've never forgotten. He said, 'Tommy, you're almost five. I think you're old enough to understand something. Everything your daddy has, he owes first to Almighty God who loves me and who gave His Son to die for me, and second to the United States of America that took me in and gave me citizenship and opportunity.

"'Son,' he went on, 'you'll never *see* God, for God is spirit. But you were made in the image of God, even if you, like all the rest of us, may distort and damage that image during your lifetime.

"'Some people have skin that is blacker than yours, some redder, some yellower, and some, like your mother, even whiter.'" (My mother is just as Anglo-Saxon as my dad is a Near-Easterner. In fact, often when I address the Daughters of the American Revolution, who can be a bit snooty at times and make me feel they are turning up their noses at my odd-sounding name, I remind them that I'm just as much a WASP as they are, on my mother's side—so Anglo-Saxon that my forebearers didn't come over on the *Mayflower*, they helped build that ship to get rid of those first 'flower people'!)

"But Dad went on, 'You'll only see God during your lifetime in the face of your fellow man. So when you love your fellow man, you are loving God; and when you do any disservice to man, you're doing disservice to God, for he, like yourself, was made in the image of God.'"

I guess the story took with those boys in Germany. I well remember that one lad came up afterward and kissed my hand. He embarrassed me, but he meant it when he said, "I came here mad. I came here to destroy; because I came with hatred. But I go away with love."

I think Bob Brown and I were able to help those boys see that their problems weren't caused by race relations, by prejudice; they were the result of classifying people as good or bad on the basis of the group they belonged to. But each of us is an individual; to be treated like one, to be accepted for what you are, you have to start the process—*you* have to accept yourself. Before you can love others as yourself, you have to love yourself.

I say to young people all over the country, if the United States, divided as we are, is ever again to be, literally, a "united states," we must learn to teach you what we are still learning—how to accept yourself as you really are. Sure, you're not as great as you dream of being; but you are a creation of God, an individual, and you are responsible for making the most of the potential that was born in you. You *must* do your own thing!

One final point about doing your own thing. Notice the action word in that phrase—you've got to *do* something. Please don't fall into the error that so many times my generation does. When called on to do something, to help in some way, they'll say, "I'm just not capable enough" or "I couldn't handle *that* job." They mean to sound humble, but I've found that usually this isn't a sign of genuine humility—it's the sound of carelessness, laziness, callousness, and cowardice.

Don't ask for responsibilities equal to your strength; trust God to give you strength equal to your responsibilities.

I think you can see why the first in my collection of the writings of Paul would be, "Do not let the world squeeze you into its mold." Surely it means as much today as when it was written.

Belonging to a group or a gang is fine so long as you don't surrender your individuality to it. It's a rare gang that will build anything; instead, gangs throw stones, so we can never isolate the persons who throw them. I'm asking that you not be with those who throw stones, but rather with those who share a concern for a cause, and pay the price of being different.

You are one of a kind . . . but what kind?

Let's move on to the second of the writings of Paul I would share with you. It is the wish, coming down through the centuries from the time of the Apostle to the present, that you and I may have joy and contentment.

Don't confuse joyousness with happiness. You see, happiness depends on happenings. Today I'm happy because I got up after a good night's rest, and my day's work is what I love doing. So of course I'm happy; who wouldn't be?

But if all we had was happiness, then we wouldn't have much great music; it has often been written by the brokenhearted. You'd never know, listening to some of Mozart's happiest and greatest music, that it was written when he was both penniless and sick; you'd never know, listening to Beethoven's gigantic *Ninth Symphony*, ending with its magnificent "Hymn to Joy," that he was deaf, totally deaf, when he wrote it—and what greater tragedy for a composer than deafness? Great poetry has come "out of the valley"; few great artists, in any form, had lives filled with what you and I would call "happiness."

No, I'm not talking about happiness, I'm talking about joy —that deepseated confidence that keeps you on an even keel whatever storms of life you have to sail through.

Here's what Paul wrote his friends at Thessalonica, in the fifth part of his first letter. Toward the close, in the sixteenth paragraph, he says, "Rejoice evermore."

That's short and simple, but it's loaded! He means, "Be a bubbling spring!" to me, because I was raised around springs, and to me they are a symbol for everlasting enthusiasm. To you, the meaning could be, "Be a magnet to lift others with your enthusiasm; it's the secret of charisma!"

But Paul doesn't stop telling you what to do; he goes on to tell you how to do it. He says next, "Pray without ceasing." Did I lose you by mentioning something as square as praying? Whether I did or whether I didn't, let me go on, because he says, "In everything give thanks, for this is the will of God in Christ Jesus concerning you." And there he wraps up a whole psychological truth in just a few words.

It works this way, and I defy you to prove me wrong! To be joyful, pray without ceasing; give thanks for everything that's happening to you. The psychological truth is that you cannot be thankful and depressed at the same time!

If I had mentioned depression to young people some years back, they'd have said, "Why bring that up—that's an adult problem." Sure, it's an adult problem, but you aren't immune. Many of you young people know what depression is; many of you are already using tranquilizers, and some of you have sampled drugs simply to escape depression. You, too, know the feelings of being put down, loneliness, and despair.

A book published three hundred years ago has a title I love: *Pills to Purge Melancholy*. And do you know what the "pills" are? It's a book of songs! Now I love music as much as anyone, but there are times when I don't feel like singing. The only sure cure I know is that you cannot be depressed and thankful in the same mind at any time.

It's easy to see how Paul's advice applies to you personally —easy to see, but sometimes hard to do, I'll admit. But let me take it a step further and apply it not just to personal problems but to the problems facing us as a nation and as citizens of a world that's constantly growing smaller.

On another of my visits to lovely Europe on behalf of the Air Force, I was speaking as I like best—completely informally, surrounded by about 400 men out on a runway. Even though the Air Force was my host, the group was about equally divided between Army and Air Force—the Army boys, draftees; the Air Force boys who had joined so they wouldn't be drafted.

When I'm speaking, you'd be surprised at how much listening I do at the same time—listening with my eyes, as well as my ears, to see how well I'm getting my points across. This time, both my eyes and my ears told me, "Some of these boys aren't with you; something's bugging them about how our country's dealing with its problems."

Right on the spot, an idea hit me, and I put it into action. I don't do things off the top of my head too much when I'm speaking; that's dangerous. Usually, mine is planned confusion. But this time I did react spontaneously. I stopped and asked, "How many of you believe that the United States has let you down?"

Out of that group of more than 400, about 20 hands went up. That's less than 5 per cent—not bad, since about 5 per cent of any group will usually tell you they believe black is white! Anyway, I turned to the nearest man with his hand up and asked him, "How did America let you down?"

He said, "Oh, Tom, I wasn't really thinking about America letting *me* down—I was thinking about so-and-so back home." He happened to come from Newark, New Jersey; and there are plenty of people in the ghettos of Newark and other cities who have a lot to complain about.

But I said, "You missed the point. I didn't ask about a relative or someone you know back home, or something you thought you saw, or anything you know by hearsay. I asked how America had let *you* down." And he said he "guessed maybe it hadn't."

I went on to the next one, and then on through about twelve, and not one had anything to say about how America had let *him* down; it was always some circumstance or another about someone else. So I asked the others, as a group, if any of them had an answer. Not one made a reply.

Since then, I've done this at most of the bases I visit, as well as on college and university campuses. Someday, someone is going to give me a first-hand answer, but so far, no one has been able to tell me how America let him down.

Well, I started off with this group of men from what was bothering them, rather than telling them what I had started to. I said, "I don't want to suggest that America is the only good nation in the world; it's my privilege to visit and speak

The Gray Beard Advises the New Beards

in a number of nations, and I find they are fine nations. But I must say that for my life style, America is the finest. I would not exchange the worst that I've experienced in our country for the best I've enjoyed in any other.

"Nor am I saying that I am blind to our faults. Flying back and forth across the United States, to the tune of 1,000 miles a day, I see our problems; and I guess because God made me so sensitive, I lose sleep over them at times. There are nights when I go to sleep broken-hearted.

"But I believe that only when you're thankful for what you have will you really want to improve it. In fact, if you aren't really thankful for some gift, you won't even do very much to save it.

"Think back to when you were a child and got two or three presents for Christmas. Say you were given three trucks—a yellow dump truck, a white panel truck and a red fire engine; and it happened that you just loved that red fire truck. When your neighborhood buddy was over playing with you, if he broke one of the other trucks you were upset, but you got over it; but let him just scratch that fire truck and bang—you hit him before he could see what was coming!

"If a wheel came off that fire truck, you'd go running to Dad for him to fix it. But it didn't much matter what happened to the others, and soon you'd drop them off the side of the steps to have a play wreck.

"But that which you liked best, the truck you were really thankful for, was the only one you took care of, and tried to preserve.

"The same thing's true in bigger things. The way I divide our youth is on this basis. There are those who are critical and just destructive; they have no thanksgiving for America. They aren't the least bit appreciative for what they've been given, so they haven't any care about just tearing down without planning how to build.

"Those who really care are the ones concerned with building. When you're thankful, you don't overlook the scratches or the broken wheel—you just work with everything you can lay your hands on, and everything within you, to repair it, improve it, perfect it.

"That's why I feel America will be benefited not by those who are only critical of her, but by those of us who are thankful for what she has given us."

Then I went on to say this: "I am part of the Establishment, and I say this to you straight out: If you're against the Establishment, you're against me. But before you take any potshots at me, let me tell you why I'm proud to be part of the Establishment.

"There had to be an established country for my father to come to—otherwise he would have found a disorganized wilderness.

"It was an established America which developed a public school system so I could receive an education. It was an established America which had freedom of religion, so my father could serve his God as a minister wherever he was called. An established America had businessmen who took part of the profits from their businesses and supported the colleges. And when I attended college, I only paid for one third of the cost; that's all tuition covers. Two thirds of your education is paid for by contributions given to the school itself—and most of those contributions come from business.

"It is established America which allows me to do every day what I enjoy doing most—speaking and sharing my thoughts.

"I would be a complete hypocrite if I were critical of the Establishment; I don't overlook its faults, but I begin by being thankful for what it has given me and made it possible for me to do on my own. And I would suggest to you that if you're going to bite the hand that feeds you, at least you should be kind enough to take out your teeth and gum it to death!"

There's one other point about being thankful that this bit of Paul's wisdom makes clear to us. Have you ever noticed that the people who are dead-serious critics, the destructive ones, have no sense of joy at all? That's not the kind of leadership I want to follow, no matter how serious their complaints or valid their criticism. My adrenalin is turned on when I see a problem and realize I can have the privilege of helping to solve it; because I'm thankful for what this country has given me and meant to me, I'm ready to pitch in and do my best to make it not just good but the best! My thankfulness makes me joyful.

I started learning to be thankful, as you'd expect, from my dad. He once suggested that each morning I start the day by writing down four things for which I am thankful; it's a practice I still follow. So, I wake up every morning and start the day by praying my simple prayer, "Oh, God, don't let me die until I'm dead." I've met too many folks who are dead, but they just haven't been buried yet. Some are 19 and are dead . . . they've given up. More are in their 40's and 50's and they're just as dead . . . they've given up, too. Thank God I know some like my dad, young and alive in their 70's. Confucius said it for me: "Some people die old at thirty, and some die young at ninety." So I pray that I'll keep on living until I die.

After praying my prayer, I write down the four things that I am thankful for that day. Many times I write the same four things I wrote yesterday; it doesn't make any difference; I'm still thankful. And writing them down makes them have a double impression on my mind, so I do it every morning.

You may well say, "Tom, you ought to be thankful—you have an easy life!"

And that's true. I know I have an easy life—probably as easy as any adult, and maybe far easier than yours. Speaking is an easy life; I get disgusted when I hear my colleagues of the podium talk about how tired they are, how hard they work, how difficult it is to get yourself up to speak every day, all the time appealing to you for sympathy. Instead, I revel in it. I get to fly about to every part of this beautiful country, meeting fascinating people wherever I go; I step into a situation, I speak and I "split"—before the audience has a chance to catch me. My creditors can't catch me; they don't even know where I am! There are a few worries; when you read the financial statements of the airlines in recent years and find yourself at 30,000 feet on a line that's losing money, in a plane that was put together by the lowest bidder, you find yourself putting real meaning into your prayers. But basically, it is an easy life. And I'm thankful that I find it easy . . . that I'm doing something I enjoy so much I can take the troubles in stride.

But my father started teaching me to be thankful back when our family might go a day without anything to eat, because there was no food in the house. The people for whom my father was pastor were prayerful and conscientious; they prayed, "Lord, you keep our preacher humble and we'll be sure to starve him to death"—and they didn't let God down on their half of the bargain! But when we had nothing to eat, Dad would have us pray and thank God we were strong enough so this wouldn't hurt us, but that we would be greater people because of it.

I do a lot of speaking for Scouting, as you may know, and people automatically assume I like to camp out. Born in a Baptist parsonage, I was born "camped out"—and I've spent my entire life trying to rise above it! I spoke at a Scout camp on one occasion, and drove 20 miles to the nearest town to

The Gray Beard Advises the New Beards

find a motel to stay in. I tell people, truly, "I won't camp out for anybody!"

Don't let me leave you thinking it was all bad; it wasn't. We even had some safety factors you don't have today; I well remember when a roaring fire broke out in the bathroom and burned it down, and the fire never even touched our house!

Seriously, it wasn't all bad, and it was when it was tough that I learned to be thankful. It's actually easier, then; if you wait until you have enough to be thankful for, you'll find that all those things you have to be thankful for only make you critical of them, and more covetous. If you're used to walking, even a jalopy rides well; if you've ridden all your life, you want to be seen in a new car or you'll stay home!

Oh, we have much to be thankful for, beginning with life itself. Maybe you've read the fascinating study of life in a concentration camp by Dr. Victor Frankl. Among other unexpected things, he points out that the death rate among newcomers to the camp was quite high at first, when those who had lost the will to live simply gave up and died. After that, the rate of suicide was lower than ours in America today. When a man is thankful for life, he fights to preserve it—even in a concentration camp. That's why I have full hope that we'll find most of our POW's and even many of the men now listed as Missing In Action still alive after the war; if the North Vietnamese give them even the least chance to live, I believe they will, for they have had much to be thankful for.

Too often, I'm afraid, we have confused love of things with love of life. We may try to be thankful for the clothes we wear, the comfortable homes we live in, the incomes our fathers make that we spend (even as we're critical of Dad and his generation). But if you can get down to basics and be thankful for the simple essentials—food, strength, good health, friendships, life itself—you'll find you have motivation for living, magnetism and charisma for leading, and a clear program of appreciation of what's right in our society and what needs changing.

You'll be interested to know that I've made my dad's suggestion for daily thanksgiving to your parents at business conventions throughout the country, and you ought to hear the comments and see the letters I've received. People tell me they've been writing down four things to be thankful for every day, and what a difference it makes—this one says in her attitude toward her home and the housework she hates; that one in his attitude toward his secretary when he walks into the office; and many, many tell me of the change in attitude they feel toward their communities and their country.

So remember the second statement of Paul: "Be joyful; pray without ceasing; in everything give thanks, for this is the will of God." The only way you can be contented, a person who draws others and has a deep-down feeling of security, is to learn to give thanks for everything, for this is God's will for your life.

The third statement I would have to include is that tremendous affirmation of faith he made to Timothy in the first part of his second letter, in the twelfth paragraph: "For I know whom I have believed, and am persuaded that He is able to keep that which I have committed unto him against that day" (the day of judgment).

You've heard a great deal about faith in your lifetime, from the sermons preached about the power of a mustard seed and the faith that moves mountains to the half-joking tag-line the late Adam Clayton Powell always used, "Keep the faith, baby!"

So here I am, offering you a quotation from Paul with the purpose of telling you to have faith; I sound like all the others, don't I? But hear me out. I'm not shouting, "Have faith, and faith will make you free," or even, "Keep the faith!" It's not just a matter of having faith; I believe you can have perfect faith in the material progress of this world and be completely, utterly lost. No, faith must have direction and goals. The question is, where is your faith headed?

That's why I like what Paul said: "I know whom I believe in," (meaning God) "and there I've lodged my faith."

Faith that leads somewhere is something that man seems to need. You may not have heard of it, but a conference has met periodically in Yugoslavia for almost a decade providing a chance for a group of philosophers from the Soviet Union to sit down and have dialogue with a group of Judeo-Christian theologians. The conference hasn't been secret, but it also hasn't been publicly announced, because of the reasonable fear that announcement would ruin any opportunity for good discussion.

One of the statements that sort of leaked out of one of the early meetings so appealed to my prejudice that I had to check it out, because I so hoped it was true. A Soviet philosopher said they were finding it increasingly difficult to build a tranquil society without giving man some help when he thinks he's done wrong (they have no word for "sin" in their vocabulary, and that pretty severely handicaps the concept of "repentance") or without some hope in life after death.

Forgiveness for our sins and hope in life after death are two of the cardinal tenets of Christianity; and here is not just anyone, but a philosopher, from the Soviet Union—a country controlled by materialism, a country ruled, at least in name, by a philosophy derived from a man who said, "Religion is nothing but an opiate for the masses"—admitting to fellow philosophers that materialism isn't enough, that man needs faith.

Do you remember when the Russian cosmonaut came back

from his first flight in space and said that he didn't find God out there? Sometimes, in talking about him, we overlook a very serious point. He was criticized for making that statement when he was visiting at the Seattle World's Fair. Yet, if my memory serves me correctly, he made the statement at the World's Fair on a Sunday morning, to a group of people who at least said they believed in God, and worshipped at their churches freely. But it was Sunday morning . . . why weren't they at church? What right had they to criticize him?

I think the Soviet philosopher who found that people need forgiveness of their sins and the hope of life eternal, and the Soviet cosmonaut who at least went looking for God in outer space, were closer to being religious, to having faith, than many of us who profess a faith but don't live it.

A true atheist isn't the person who says, every time you ask him, "There is no God." The true, and destructive, kind of atheism is when we say, "God, God!" with our lips, but live without a commitment to our God.

I have known avowed atheists who have lived according to all the precepts of Christianity; indeed, I've known more than one who taught Sunday school in our churches; and all I can say is that it is more difficult for them to live as they do, without faith, than it is for us to follow the same precepts with faith.

When I say that you must have a meaningful faith, echoing Paul, it is with the hope that you might have the inner security that comes when you feel God within you. I know God is within each of His creations; when you feel the security of that knowledge, you can become the creative, alive person you are capable of becoming, because God, through you, is living and serving out His purposes.

A friend suggested I read a book by William Irwin Thompson called, *At the Edge of History*. I wanted to read it because Mr. Thompson was born in 1937, which makes him a little younger than I, and is considered a liberal; I thought it would be good to read a book by a man who would not appeal to my prejudices, but who might make my thinking go in a different direction than usual. He did.

Mr. Thompson said something like this: The hippie goes out, puts a coin in the fusebox, short-circuits the wires, and says, "I've got light!" The revolutionary goes out, burns down the building, and dances and sings, "I've got light!" The Establishment goes out and says, "Where did my forebearers go wrong? Why didn't they provide enough light?" (And if you happened to be in New York during the famous "black-out" or anywhere on the East Coast during the more recent "brown-outs," you know with what eloquence and with how many variations the Establishment made that and other less printable comments.)

Mr. Thompson said that if there is hope for America, it is not the hippie, with his coin short-circuit, nor with the revolutionary burning down the building, nor with the Establishment condemning their forebearers. He said he found the answer, not in his search within the quasi-Christian community in which he was raised in the United States, but more in his studies of the life style of the mystics of the Far East.

We make a basic error, according to Mr. Thompson, in talking about passing on the light as though it is a torch, that can go from hand to hand or from generation to generation. The only real light, Mr. Thompson says, is the light that comes from the soul, the inner light . . . the light that lets you know that God is present, for He is light . . . the light we can trust as we walk as much as that light that comes from without and guides our path.

Mr. Thompson and the Apostle Paul were talking about the same thing, weren't they?

My own commitment can be summed up in two poems.

The first, the famous "Invictus", by William Ernest Henley; the second, an answer to it entitled, "My Captain", by Dorothea Day.

INVICTUS

Out of the night that covers me
Black as the pit from pole to pole,
I thank whatever gods may be
For my unconquerable soul.

In the fell clutch of circumstance
I have not winced nor cried aloud;
Under the bludgeonings of chance
My head is bloody, but unbowed.

Beyond this place of wrath and tears
Looms but the Horror of the shade;
And yet the menace of the years
Finds, and shall find, me unafraid.

It matters not how straight the gate,
How charged with punishments the scroll;
I am the master of my fate;
I am the captain of my soul.

—W. E. Henley

MY CAPTAIN

Out of the light that dazzles me,
Bright as the sun from pole to pole,
I thank the God I know to be
For Christ the conqueror of my soul.

Since His the sway of circumstance
I would not wince nor cry aloud.
Under that rule which men call chance
My head with joy is humbly bowed.

> Beyond this place of sin and tears—
> That life with Him! and His aid
> That, 'spite the menace of the years,
> Keeps, and shall keep, me unafraid.
>
> I have no fear though strait the gate;
> He cleared from punishments the scroll;
> Christ is the Master of my fate,
> Christ is the Captain of my soul.
>
> —Dorothea Day

There you have the beginning of my compilation of the writings of St. Paul, in this year of grace 1972—writings that Paul set down in the year 41 A.D. and later—and they are just as meaningful and needed for today's changing youth as they were in that time.

And here's another old gray beard speaking to you, the new beard (if you're a clean-shaven boy or an ever-unbearded girl, forgive me my play on words). I have this to say to you: "Don't be a copy of my generation; but at the same time, don't fall into the trap of being a carbon copy of your generation. Don't let the world squeeze you into the mold; rather, find your own individuality through God. You are truly and wonderfully created as an individual; live it!"

Second, I would say, "Clear the cobwebs from your thinking; gain the magnetism, the charisma, that comes from true thankfulness. When you have found peace within you, others will be attracted to find the secret from you."

Finally, I tell you to have faith, and know what that faith means to you. If you want to be fresh and creative, find for yourself that Huxley spoke the truth when he said, "Inside each of us is a God-shaped void that must be filled only by the eternal God."

You are changing; you are young, and you are changing. The world is changing. I'm the gray beard; I'm glad, but

I'm afraid. I'm not going to flatter you by saying that with folks like you we can make a good world. I don't know. I don't know if you're man enough, whatever your sex. I don't know if you're strong enough to know you can't do it by yourself.

I don't know if you're willing to pay the price.

I do know if you will truly *do* your thing, if you'll be thankful, and if you'll allow the source of eternal strength to flow through you, then we can change the world for the better.

But short of that, I'm not sure. It's up to you.

Yes, it's really up to you.

Prefix to Chapter IV

THE DREAM OF A PERFECT WORLD

This speech has been delivered to more than 200 high school groups in America and to many college groups as well. It encompasses my own personal philosophy on work. I think I am basically lazy, and I know I need to be constantly inspired to work. In this speech, I try to sum up the things that were said to me, the things I wish had been said to me stronger, and the things I need to say, all on my own, about the importance of work.

The speech has been given before the National 4-H Club conventions, the National Order of the Arrow (one of Scouting's high honors), and it has gone around the world because I've been privileged to speak before the high schools for dependents of United States Air Force personnel at bases all over the globe. Before I could use it before these audiences, it had to be approved by the "brass"—not so they could censor it, but because I'm a minister, they had to be sure whatever I had to say didn't get into the gray area of government support for religion. Apparently, they feel this speech doesn't do that, but that it fills a need for youth today.

IV. The Dream of a Perfect World

H. G. Wells, the famous British writer, always believed in the possibility of a Utopia. Throughout his life, he dreamed of a perfect world. But he did more than just dream; he worked for it. Believing in the importance of having *everybody* learn from history, he turned from writing novels to a task no historian would dare attempt and wrote an *Outline of History* —a history of the world! Many historians sneered at it, but the people for whom he wrote it—the common people—bought it by the millions, and read it and learned from it.

Mr. Wells knew our world wasn't perfect, but he knew what had to be done. He suggested that the perfect world would come about whenever the young people of a single generation decided to use their God-given abilities to their fullest.

That's a truism it's impossible to argue with, although as we watch the news on TV, listen to our transistors or read our newspapers, it is difficult, even in our wildest imaginations, to envision a perfect world. Still, I think we can agree that the world would be a better place if we just used the abilities and the capabilities that we have.

You remember a story that Jesus told, a simple story like all his parables, about commerce and business—but with a spiritual application. A businessman with large holdings served as the chairman of a conglomerate. An occasion came up where he needed to travel to a foreign country, so he called in the three divisional presidents of his corporation to go over their responsibilities while he was gone. One had five companies under his direction; the second had two companies under his supervision; while the third was guiding the direction of one company.

When he returned, he called in each of the executives and asked, "How was business while I was away?"

The head of the largest division said, "Sir, I think I did pretty well; I was able to double our profits while you were gone."

The chairman nodded and said, "Boy, that's great! It's good to have you at my right hand."

The president with two companies came in and reported, "While you were gone, I'm happy to report that in my companies I doubled our profits." And the chairman gave him, also, well-deserved praise.

The president of the third division reported, "Sir, you're a funny man. Sometimes you expect to reap where you've never even sown. Though you have been a genius in building your business, and very successful, you've always been very difficult to work for—you know that; and you know you've got a reputation for a terrible temper. I couldn't take the risk of your wrath, and I certainly didn't want to let you down; so I turned to the banker for counsel. I told him we just wanted to be sure I had the company report to show you, exactly like it was when you went away. I knew I was passing up any chance for profits, but I thought you'd want to be protected against any possibility of a loss. So that's the way things are—we're exactly where we were when you left."

The chairman turned in wrath to the president with five companies and said, "Get rid of this man! He's fired! I don't need him; now I'll divide the operation and responsibilities he's had between you and my other trusted executive."

There are several things about this story that have always bugged me. One is that the chairman could have promoted three men and had two of the three succeed. Any time you can get two out of three to be winners, that's a good batting

The Dream of a Perfect World 105

average. Most of us would do well if we could bat .333—never mind .667!

But the language the chairman used is shocking. He didn't say, "Give him another chance. Let's see if we've placed him wrong and he ought to be in another job that would make use of his talents." He didn't even talk about severance pay. He simply said, "Get rid of him! I don't need him." The chairman wasn't reacting to the position of the president because he had only one company; *it was because he didn't do anything with what was entrusted to him.*

Marcus Aurelius had it right when he said, "Dig within thee, there lies a fount of good . . . a fount that will forever well up if thou wilt forever dig."

Each of us has his own abilities. You're not responsible for living up to the capabilities of your neighbor; you're only responsible for your own. You don't have to make all A's because the student next to you makes all A's or has a 4.0 average; you're only responsible for that kind of average if your abilities allow you to be able to do the same thing. But you *must* use what you have!

The Bible puts much emphasis on small things . . . the widow's mite, a drink of cold water. The point is simple: It's not the *amount* you give; it's *how*—willingly or grudgingly—and the dedication with which you give. Many times winners and great people are handicapped; they know how to get better than how to give. Yet I've seen people we would think of as being handicapped excel, as people, beyond many who had normal physical or mental gifts.

No wonder great men have felt the importance of this story to Jesus. Carlyle thundered it as a law of life, like those Moses brought down from Mount Sinai: "This is the question of questions—what talent is born in you and how do you employ it?" Dr. Johnson prayed, with a gentle modesty in his strength, that, "When I shall render up at the last day an account of the talent committed to me, I shall receive pardon for the sake of Jesus Christ." Macauley remarked that this parable had given to the English language a new adjective, "talented."

In this one story is the whole basis of whether you're a success—not judged by outward appearances but by the inner judgments that allow you to feel contented and satisfied that you have given your best. All of your life depends on whether you use that with which you're entrusted or fumble your opportunities away.

But *why* did this man fail? I've found four reasons; each is a very human failing that you or I are as liable to as he was. I think it's very bad psychology to use negatives when talking with anybody, and very bad taste to use them with young people. But in explaining my four reasons why this man failed, I'm going to use negatives; and out of them, I hope and pray for a positive result.

I. A Lust for Laziness

I think even a casual observer would feel that the man who failed was not as ambitious as the two who succeeded and also that his lack of ambition was due to laziness. That's a fault any man may have, but it's one I've found too often among the young.

Understand me when I say you're lazy; I want you to know what I'm saying before you throw your books at me. I am not saying that you do not have energy, but the difference between having energy and having ambition is in whether or not the energy is harnessed and directed. When it is, it becomes ambition.

You have both energy and knowledge. Far more aware of the world about you than most of my generation were when we were ten years older than you are now, you've had the whole world brought to your fingertips. But the question isn't

The Dream of a Perfect World

simply what you've got; what's important is, "How do you use your energy and your knowledge?"

There's a basic law of nature that literally scares me. It is: WHAT YOU DON'T USE, YOU LOSE.

If you put your right arm in a sling and leave it there for 12 months, you'll have to learn to write all over again when you take it out. Put your left leg in a cast. Leave it there for a year. Take it off, and you'll have to learn to walk again. What you don't use, you lose.

Therefore, the talents and abilities you and I have entrusted to us will be corroded by disuse and eventually impossible to use unless we put them to work in hopeful and helpful endeavor.

A second law of nature, closely in line with this, scares me almost as much: STOP AND I'LL KILL YOU.

If you can stop something from growing, it immediately begins to die. Put a string around a rose bush; keep it from spreading out its canes and branches and roots, and it begins to die. Put a cellophane envelope around a rose bud; keep it from spreading its petals and it, too, begins to die.

Uncertainty can strangle a human life just as surely as the cellophane strangles the rose bud. We cannot just float along, trying to find a way to fulfillment by blind luck; unfortunately, nature doesn't give us time to just sit back and hope the right opportunity will open up in front of us.

Put these two laws of nature together and you'll understand the importance of work. My definition of work is: "the avenue of expression for the abilities that God has entrusted to each of us." Remember, if those abilities aren't used, we lose them; if we wait to use them, they'll die. And when young people appear to be perfectly content to get, and to go on getting, rather than to give; when you seem willing to waste your abilities by not putting them to work, my generation immediately generalizes and says, "Young people today are just plain lazy!"

Not so much in your defense as in explanation, there is a reason many of you do appear to be lazy. We have misunderstood, or failed to notice, a crucial difference between your generation and ours. It's obvious, and I guess that's why we overlooked it. You have a different reason for working than we did.

All it took to get my generation to go to work was an opportunity. We were hungry, and we needed things. So we weren't too concerned about what the job was; we were concerned about how much it would pay and how soon we could draw a paycheck. We needed a job for survival.

You're not so much concerned about this because you have always been fed and clothed; you have lived all your lives in at least relatively good times. You haven't felt the necessity of work for survival, so you feel work should offer fulfillment, not be just a means to an end.

That's an important change, a fundamental change; and it's important that you understand we are the first society that has ever existed that is so rich we can afford to concern ourselves about whether work is fulfilling or not. Most men who ever lived before our time, and most men alive today who do not live in America, have had to do whatever work they could find simply to stay alive. No wonder Thoreau wrote, "Most men lead lives of quiet desperation." You see this need not be so, and you are not content with work without fulfillment. Now we can afford that attitude, but it is brand new. It is a fundamental change.

There's no better way this is reflected than in the way we enlist you into employment.

Even as recently as 1963, when I left the pastorate and started full-time speaking to employer groups, I would tell them that the way to hire a man for a job was to spell out the

The Dream of a Perfect World

job in detail. Specify what was to be done, what experience or preparation was necessary, and what it would pay; set up a Job Performance Graph to indicate whether or not the job was being done to specification. If a man didn't meet the requirements, he was fired.

Only half a dozen years ago I realized that this procedure was wrong and started using a whole series of new suggestions. It pleases me to find these suggestions have been well backed by the Harvard Graduate School of Business and many others. Now, when we seek to employ you, we ask three questions:

1. What would you like to do?

2. How committed are you to what you would like to do?

3. (And this is rather solicitous on our part) How can I help you do what you want to do?

I don't want you to think this means an employer isn't hiring you to get a job done; he is, and he must, and you've got to do that job or he'll have to fire you. But this set of questions helps make sure that when you are hired, *you* will get some satisfaction out of the job you have to do; and we understand that only when a job gives you some fulfillment are you going to be content with it.

So these three questions actually put you on the spot. Why would you be interested in becoming part of a particular company? And if you are interested, how conscientious and honest are you in your commitment? Then, how can the company make you feel even more fulfilled, so it builds loyalty on your part?

By putting this kind of emphasis on you and your satisfaction during the hiring process, an employer lets you see more than just what part your job plays in the process of turning out whatever the company makes; you can also begin to see how the product or service the company provides makes for a better life for people, and how the profits from the company help improve the community. And when you understand these aspects of business, I believe you will see what many of us have known but have done a poor job of conveying to you —that the corporations of America have been the backbone of the good life that makes our country head and shoulders above the other nations of the world, even with all our faults.

But you should also understand that, because this change in attitude toward work is so new, it isn't always easy for those of us who were brought up with the old attitude to feel comfortable with the new. It dawns on me that my children can get—or be given—almost anything easier than I could get a drink of water when I was a small child.

No, I'm not being facetious. In the parsonage where we lived in southwestern Pennsylvania, our water came from a spring over the side of the hill. Every morning my brothers had to go down to the basement and pump for an hour to get water from the spring up into a cistern in the house so we could use it for bathing, cooking, drinking and so on.

That pumping wasn't easy, but it was necessary. My children—thank God—have never known even that kind of necessity. Sure, they've always had chores to do around the house; but they haven't had to work to earn, or even to drink. My children can get almost anything easier than I could get a drink of water.

You look at work not as something to keep you alive but as something that keeps you alive emotionally and even spiritually, as well as economically. Maybe this explains why, in all of our surveys, we find that you never put salary as the most important consideration in finding a job.

But just because you have higher expectations of what a job

The Dream of a Perfect World 111

will provide you, just because you feel work must give you fulfillment, don't forget that you also have to fulfill the job. While work must satisfy you, you also have to satisfy your employer; no change in attitude toward work is going to change that fundamental fact of economic life. So remember that the first fault of the president who failed was laziness; whatever else he got out of *his* job, he didn't do the job he was hired to do. We now expect you to have ambition for more than economic satisfaction—but we expect your other ambitions to be in addition to, not replacements for, your ambition to get the job done.

II. A Passion for Popularity

Remember what the president who failed said to the chairman? He was very honest; he said, "I couldn't take the risk of your wrath." He wanted to stay on the good side of the chairman; so rather than do anything wrong, he did nothing. He paid a high price for trying to stay popular.

You should want to be popular; and after looking into the faces of many, many young people, I imagine you are. But remember something very important: there is a vast difference between popularity and respect.

By trying to remain popular with the chairman, the president who failed lost his respect. The same thing can happen to any of us.

Tragically enough, often the things you do to try to make yourself popular are the very things that cause you to lose respect.

Popularity is a fickle mistress that can turn very quickly from one favorite to a new one, leaving the old one wondering, "What happened?" Respect is built on knowledge of the real, inner *you*, knowledge that makes those around you trust and admire you. Popularity is a surface thing, usually. It results in having people say nice things *to* you; respect is reflected in what they think about you when you're not around. Popularity can cause you to make a fool of yourself to get acceptance; earning respect may require you to risk dislike in order to be worthy of trust.

Let me give you a corny illustration, but a real one. During my junior year at North High School in Binghamton, New York, we played our cross-town rival, Central High School, for the Baseball Conference Championship. The rivalry was so bitter that the usual agreement was that the team that won the game lost the rock fight afterward.

Going into the top half of the seventh inning, we had a one-run lead; and because the field wasn't lighted, we played only seven inning games. So if we could hold our lead through just the next three outs, we would not only have beaten our cross-town rivals but have the Conference Championship as a bonus.

Their first batter, a right hander, came up, swung late and dumped the ball behind the first baseman. As you know, if you can push the ball to the opposite field, you have a stand-up double, at least—and that's what he had. The next batter hit a short single into center field. Well, I knew my center fielder had one of the best arms of any outfielder I'd ever played with; so if the runner tried to score, we ought to nail him at the plate.

He did try to score; he didn't even break stride coming around third, with the coach waving him on in. Our center fielder scooped up the ball and threw it to me at the plate in one perfect motion. I had it in plenty of time to block the plate, move down the line and tag the runner out by a country mile.

Now remember, I was a preacher's kid; and people often have funny ideas about how preachers' kids ought to act, and even talk. So, wanting my gang to think I was one of them, I not only put the ball on the runner in a way that he'd

The Dream of a Perfect World

remember, I also said, "I got you that time!" But I didn't stop there; I had to add, "I got you that time—you damn fool!"

I thought this would make me look good. I was proving I could use the Anglo-Saxon four-letter monosyllables as well as the next guy on the team; they'd know I was really one of them.

But when I got back to the bench, all my coach said was, "Tom, I'm sorry for you." And from then on, I never had the same respect from the rest of the team that I'd had before.

It wasn't that the word "damn" was either that good or that bad; some people use it and never think of it as a curse word. My point is that my team members knew I could use better English than that to express myself; by trying to do something to earn their popularity, I lost their respect.

Being the catcher and a fairly decent ballplayer, I was looked to for leadership. Any of them would have used that word—and much stronger ones. But they had admired me because I didn't, and they didn't want me to lower myself to their usage just to be popular.

The same thing can happen very easily in anyone's life, but especially with you girls. Because despite Women's Lib, we still live with a double standard; and this makes it tough. We're always tougher on the girls than on the boys.

Along comes the guy whose only argument is the cliche, older than the hills, "Everybody's doing it." Or the clincher of all times, "If you really love me, you'll prove it." You want to be "in the group." But don't forget that that which can make you "in" can also make you a conversation piece in the locker room—just another tarnished trophy, used, and marked up as an "easy score," with no possibility of respect in the future.

The basis of love is mutual respect. When, instead, love is a kind of popularity contest that requires compromise, it cannot be built on respect.

Let me go a step farther and say that any time someone asks you to do something which goes against the teaching of your home, the teaching of your church or the teaching of your school—on the basis that doing it will make you popular—it would be well to just back off and see if you're not being used. You'll probably see, after you've backed off, that someone wants you to fulfill a selfish gratification; usually, you'll find that the person wants to use you, because his (or her) own insecurity demands he bring you down to his level!

One of the tough things about talking with you about the difference between popularity and respect is that it appears, at times, that we've even built the religious structure of our day on popularity rather than respect.

An illustration of what I mean—and it well may be an innocent victim, as well—is our Dr. Billy Graham, the religious giant of the contemporary scene.

Never has an American religious leader been as popular, or more exposed to the public; and it is surely not his fault that while his revivals have drawn literally millions of people, and he has reached many times more over television, our crime rate has gone unchecked, the moral tone of America has decayed, and church attendance continues to decline annually.

But what I'm talking about here is that in our zeal to reach people, we have used Madison Avenue techniques and appealed to people to make decisions, even for Christ, on the basis that, "Everybody's doing it!" Sometimes we "prime the pump" in evangelistic crusades by having what you would call "set-up converts" ready and waiting to come down the aisles, to set an example for others. You young people see through all this, and I know you turn away wondering, sometimes, if there's anything to Christianity that challenges you, or whether it's just the popular thing to do.

The Dream of a Perfect World

This is where we've misjudged you; we were trying to make the church more popular; but in so doing, we've just turned you off to it more completely.

You *want* that which makes you "Dare to be a Daniel, Dare to stand alone, Dare to have a purpose firm, Dare to make it known!"

Don't be too harsh on us; our rating service, like the ones that measure the success of television programs, is based on quantity, not quality . . . by the number of listeners or endorsers, not how deeply and well they hear the message.

We have been trying to make it *appear* that there is real credence, real faith, behind our witness; but you are right. Jesus didn't perform His supreme act of redemption when the crowds were shouting His name and He would have increased his popularity unbelievably; nor when the Devil tempted Him and He could have proved He was the Son of God; but when even His disciples had fled and He alone gave His life.

I compliment our young "Jesus People" for rejecting the popular Jesus and seeking instead the respected Jesus.

A young person came to me with what I think is a pretty good illustration of what I'm talking about. This young man was raised, as most of us were, to attend church—not believing the church is perfect, but believing that regular worship as part of the "body of Christ," which is what the church really is, is necessary. So he was taught that he was not to miss church; he was not to "sleep in" while away at prep school, that Sunday was to be honored.

On a number of occasions at school, he attended religious meetings which tried to add a popular appeal to the message of Jesus; among the speakers were people with special appeal to a young person—professional athletes. They were, and are, fine men, and I'm not putting them down; but they made their living playing football on the day this young man had been taught to honor. He felt they were endorsing Jesus just as they might endorse Gillette blades or Special 'K' for breakfast or Vitalis!

Furthermore, there was no way for him to attend church, have lunch and still get to a Sunday afternoon football game on time; he felt they were compromising themselves by playing on Sunday, and asking him to compromise himself by skipping church to see them play!

Now I understand the players' compromise; they have no choice but to play on Sunday. I can respect a man like Sandy Koufax, who always asked not to have to pitch on his Sabbath, but he could play baseball any day of the week. With the exception of some night games, most pro football is played on Sunday afternoon; and any player who wanted to respect *his* Sabbath would have to resign from his team.

But my friend had a point, and it's a point that does trouble me.

On the one hand, here's the church usually in the forefront of support of what I consider to be antiquated "blue laws" restricting people's activities on Sunday (and I've been highly criticized because I don't support those laws), then turning around and both honoring and using the witness of people who make their living playing football on Sunday.

Each professional athlete has to answer for himself before God. Since I'm an old "jock" myself, I'm pleased to call many pros in many sports my friends. I'm not acting as judge and jury . . . but I do think maybe we have overstated our case in trying to popularize Jesus. What you want, and I'm joyous that you do, is that Jesus be respected because of the demands he places on us.

No matter how carried away we get in trying to make Jesus the winner of a popularity contest, the demands He

The Dream of a Perfect World

placed on us are still stringent and rugged. If they are popular, fine; they cannot earn popularity by compromise.

The second reason the president failed is easy to see and easy to understand; it's hard to put into practice the lesson it teaches. You must decide how you will live; and all I can do is pray you will choose not that which will bring you popularity, but that which will bring you respect.

III. A Fear of Failure

I guess this reason for the president's failure makes me angrier than anything else. You have to give him credit, though; he spelled it out. He was afraid he would lose that which had been entrusted to him, and rather than risk failing, he did nothing.

Every time I see this happen, it makes me angry. I've seen a fellow strike out before he left the dugout because he *knew* the pitcher had a fast ball he couldn't hit . . . and he didn't. I've seen basketball games lost in the closing moments where that one good shot would have won. Here's a guard with a clear shot—but he's so afraid of missing and being the goat that he passes the ball off—to the tall center who's already double-teamed. The gun goes off; and the ballgame is over; and I'm fuming with anger!

I remember a football game I heard reported over the radio by a high school announcer; here's how he called one play:

"There's the snap, and the quarterback gives the ball to his left halfback. Smith's going for the right side . . . he's broken over the line behind the big tackle . . . now he's past the linebacker and only the safety can get him! Now the safety's knocked out of the play, and Smith's in the clear! He's at the 40 . . . the 50 . . . now the 40 . . . now the 30 . . . now the 20—he's down!" Then a pause . . . "It must be the result of self-tackle-ization!"

Smith was so afraid he wouldn't score that he didn't; he was so afraid he'd fall, he did. And I've seen more halfbacks stumble before they're tackled at the line of scrimmage!

When it happens in sports, it's dramatic; but that isn't the only way it can happen. How many school elections have you seen where there was only one candidate—because everybody else who might have run was afraid to lose?

And there are even more common ways the fear of failure can trip you up. Haven't you ever sat in class and been pretty sure you knew the answer to a question; but instead of raising your hand and taking a chance, you simply whispered the answer under your breath. Then the fellow next to you, who's never insulted a book by cracking it, hasn't anything to lose so he raises his hand. The teacher, after she gets over the shock of having him volunteer, calls on him; and wonder of wonders, he's right! She compliments him, of course, and makes a note in the grade book; and you sit there kicking yourself and thinking, "Old Dumb-dumb didn't know it—*I* knew it—he just heard what I whispered."

Old Dumb-bumb deserves the credit the teacher gave him; he wasn't afraid to fail.

I'm sure you've known kids who were into the drug scene; do you see how the fear of failure works in their case?

One of the biggest reasons for the prevalence of drug abuse, I'm convinced, is because of the prevalence of "copouts" —people so afraid they'll fail in the real world they need a way of instant gratification that gives them a world where they feel big without going through the process of growing big.

The problem of drug abuse isn't what it does to you physically (as bad as that is; "speed" and heroin *do* kill, and LSD and some of the others can leave lasting ill-effects); the real problem is what drug abuse does to you mentally. They all have one thing in common; they're the copout's crutch because they make you say, "I don't give a damn about anyone else; *I'm* King! I don't need anyone else; I'm King!" You don't need to do anything to prove yourself worthy of being King; just take a puff, take a sniff, take a snort, take a shot, and there you are—instant King, every time (only it doesn't work every time; and soon you're puffing, or sniffing, or snorting, or shooting because you need to get away . . . not to become King, but just to get away.)

That way of avoiding failure is a failure itself, and anyone who tries to claim his pseudo-superiority under the influence of drugs is doomed to failure in the long run.

Anyone can run away. I challenge you to have enough guts to face life without a pill or a sniff or a needle.

THANK GOD FOR FOOLS

Thank God for fools—for men who dare to dream
Beyond the lean horizon of their days;
Men not too timid to pursue the gleam
To unguessed lands of wonder and amaze.

Thank God for fools! The trails that ring the world
Are dark with blood and sweat where they have passed.
They are the flags of every crag unfurled;
Theirs—ashes and oblivion at last.

Thank God for fools—abused, of low estate.
We rear our temples on the stones they laid.
Ours is the prize their tired souls might not wait;
Theirs—the requiem of the unafraid.

The fear of failure sometimes masks itself as prudence, and only a man other men call a fool will venture where the prudent do not dare. But Anatole France said it right when he wrote, "The world has been saved by its madmen."

Henry Hudson persisted in pushing on in the search for

the Northwest Passage between Europe and the Orient even after his men mutinied; he pushed them on till they were ice-locked for the winter. In the spring, they mutinied again and set him, his son, and seven men still loyal to him adrift in their small boat; he was never seen again. But his discoveries opened Canada to further exploration; both the Hudson River in New York and Hudson's Bay in Canada are named for him. Just a few years ago the route he pioneered was proved possible; he *had* discovered the way to the Northwest Passage.

Samuel F. B. Morse was a respected artist; but he was called a lunatic when he appeared before nine different sessions of Congress, pleading for funds to build a telegraph between Baltimore and Washington. Eight times they jeered him from their presence; they were too busy with the affairs of state to listen to some madman talk about sending messages through wires. The ninth session finally gave him a small grant, just to get rid of him, I think. His invention worked, and men called him a genius; but he had long been thought a fool, and he persisted in spite of what many men would have called failure.

Cyrus Field attempted to put an undersea cable between New York and London for 13 years, with 11 different crews. The first cable completed actually operated, then failed in just three weeks. He raised new capital and kept trying, despite the popular opinion that no cable could withstand the pressure and other hazards of the ocean deeps. When he finally succeeded, he was praised on both sides of the ocean for having persisted where so many other men could see only folly and failure. One reason our nations have stood side by side is that he tied us together; it is a tribute to the fact that he didn't fear failure.

When Alexander Graham Bell came to the Philadelphia

Centennial in 1876 and talked about a little apparatus in which you could talk at one end and listen from the other end, and have your voice carry across miles, people simply dismissed him as someone who had taken leave of his senses. Now the phone lines that link New York and San Francisco, Chicago and New Orleans, and most of all, your home to the homes of your friends, prove that he wasn't afraid of being called a fool, or a failure.

The Wright brothers and their sister were thought crazy because they insisted man could fly like the birds; and as I zoom around this nation and world to the tune of 1,000 miles a day, I thank God they weren't afraid of failure.

Charles Goodyear invested 11 years of his life searching for the secret of making rubber tough and not sticky; he started when he was in jail for debt after his earlier business failed. Only his wife had faith in him; everyone else said he was a fool. Yet he invented vulcanizing; and as my tires sing on the highway, I bless him for having persisted in his folly and not fearing failure.

The list could go on and on . . . Fulton's first steamship was called "Fulton's Folly" because everybody *knew* you couldn't power a ship with steam. When Henry Ford came out with his "Tin Lizzie," my colleagues of the cloth went to their pulpits and cried out against a man who would destroy civilization. Of course, they may have been true prophets after all; they may have foreseen the way you drive!

The slogan of the young people today is, "Do your own thing." It sounds like fun, but it means that at times you have to stand alone. And doing your own thing also means not quitting. These are the lessons we have to learn from my list of great men who did *their* own thing.

Oh, sure, all of us want to quit at one time or another. I remember going home when I was in the tenth grade and telling Dad I wanted to quit school. I had what I thought was an excellent reason—the money I could earn would help the whole family.

You know what my father did? He just explained to me, in "de-tail," that I wasn't a quitter; and after that explanation, I understood it. I never thought about it again.

The thought of quitting you can't prevent; it's normal. The act of quitting you can't afford. It's not enough for me to remind you of fearless pioneers of the past; I demand you sense the loneliness of pioneering today. Our frontiers are no longer physical; our pioneers are now exploring the quality of life and how to preserve individuality in the jungle of technology.

A major difference between today and yesterday is that yesterday, only a few had to have the courage to find the frontiers and push them back; today, all have to be pioneers and have the courage to persist in spite of the fear of failure.

I find many of you have hazy ideas of what has to be done, but you're content just to rap about them among yourselves without pursuing either knowledge or action to do something. George Ward declares: "The younger generation is no longer sure it has a future." I don't buy that; you're alive, aren't you? Are you going to take whatever comes, dead before you're declared so? The ecologists don't scare me; I'm not afraid that you'll choke to death, but that you'll die before you waken.

Don't accuse us of hypocrisy while you practice it. One side of your mouths demands recognition while the other side says, "What can I do—I'm yours."

What have you done *today* to improve your home, your school or your community?

Sure, whatever you come up with won't make a big difference; but if it makes any difference at all, that's progress. And

The Dream of a Perfect World

maybe it won't work at all. But that's no reason for not trying. Only when there is a possibility of losing is there a chance of winning!

IV. An Incomplete Commitment

The final reason I think the president in the parable failed is that he wasn't sufficiently committed to his job; if he had been, his commitment would have given him the strength to overcome his weaknesses and do his job.

You can't help it if you're lazy; maybe you were just not born with a strong ambition, and no one trained it into you. You really can't help it if you have "rabbit ears," and anything anyone says can disturb you; and it's too difficult for you to give up trying to be popular by paying the price for respect. And you really can't help it if you're a coward and afraid of failing. But if nothing else works, the one thing that should keep you going is your sense of commitment.

If you have proper commitment, it will drive you and motivate you to overcome the laziness that is born in every one of us; if you have proper commitment, you're not going to let anything interfere with the usefulness of your life and tarnish the respect you've earned; if you have proper commitment, you'd rather fail trying than not have tried at all.

What is a proper commitment? It means, basically, a sense of debt. It means giving of yourself to honor your debts. What kind of debts?

Maybe I'm wrong, but the way I divide you, right across the board, between good and bad is not based on the grades you make, or how you dress, or whether your hair is long or short. I separate the sheep from the goats, the good from the bad, by how frequently you say "Thank you"—and mean it.

It took me a long while to learn how to do this. It took me

quite a while to realize that my folks deserved my thanks. As much as I wanted to be critical and claim that they didn't understand me (maybe they didn't, but probably they did; and if they didn't, it was most likely because I didn't want to be understood—and besides, I made no attempt to understand them), it finally dawned on me that my folks took care of me when I couldn't take care of myself.

My mother cooked our meals; she took care of my clothes; she stayed up all night when I was sick. Nobody paid her to do it, least of all me. Dad worked so we could have a home, and food, and clothes, and everything else. It took me a long while to understand that there was no way I could repay what they had done for me, willingly and without question—but that I owed them a reasonable sense of thanks.

Let me be corny and ask you directly: When was the last time you looked your mother and your father straight in the eye and just said, "Thank you"?

Let's go a step farther. When was the last time you thanked your teachers for their care and their concern?

Now I have a confession. I always liked school. You hear speakers get up and try to make you feel good by saying they didn't like school; well, I liked it!

I also liked to make good grades. I wasn't too smart, but I figured I had to be there 12 years anyway, so why sit in the back of the room and sulk? Unless they made us sit alphabetically, I always sat in the front row and looked as if I was paying attention, even if my mind was a thousand miles away. I convinced my teachers that, "I really want to learn"; that put me already on first base. When you've got brains that are weak *and* a nose like mine, you have to think this way!

But even liking school, it took me a long while to finally get a chance to go back and thank my teachers. I did, though, and thanked my first grade teacher, Mrs. Whitcomb (what a good name for a Massachusetts teacher!—and what a teacher!).

The Dream of a Perfect World

Even after she had to retire, at age seventy, she continued to do substitute teaching—until she was in her eighties, I understand.

I went back to thank Mrs. Whitcomb because she taught me two things: to read and to write. That sounds simple enough; but with just that basis, I could have educated myself. It would have been much more difficult, but I could have done it; many, many others have done so, and many still are doing it.

I don't mean she just taught me to be able to extract the meaning from "See Dick. See Dick run." She taught me to *want* to read. I have no trouble today reading a book in a day or a day and a half because she taught me to really want to read . . . and the whole world is in books.

She also taught me to *want* to write. That is, she gave me pride in both the construction of sentences and penmanship. I am told that I am one of the few ministers who, when I write you a note, you don't have to take it to a druggist to have it translated.

It dawned on me that Mrs. Whitcomb wasn't paid enough to do this. She did it because her reward was in imparting part of her life to her students; and actually, I was carrying around within me an investment of her very life.

From Mrs. Whitcomb I went to Mrs. Brooks, to Mrs. Hayden, and on to the other teachers I had in grade school. And how happy I was just last year when I was granted the privilege of speaking at a banquet honoring George Tate, the principal of Binghamton's North High School, on his retirement. That was an opportunity to say thanks to him and my other high school teachers. And I still stay in touch with Gene Looper, the man who not only taught me political science but also gave me a real thirst for philosophy at Furman University.

I've been lucky; I've been able to go back, as an adult, and express to my teachers my appreciation for all their investments in me, to let them know I understood my debt to them, and give them some payment in the only currency available to me—my thanks.

You're lucky; you're closer to your teachers. When was the last time you said "Thank you" to them?

Also, I thanked my country. It may sound funny, but finally I realized what it meant to be born in this country . . . my dad was born overseas in bondage, while I was born in Kalamazoo, Michigan, in freedom. Each day I get to do my "thing," and each day I should give thanks for the country that makes this possible.

I sat down and wrote a letter to the President of the United States. What wastebasket it ended up in, I'll never know. But I wanted to thank the United States, and the only way I knew to do this was to write the man who was serving as our leader, the President.

But most of all, I thank my Creator. Through my God, by faith in Jesus Christ, my whole life has its beginning, its ending, as well as everything in between. I'm grateful for that day when, as a lad in Pennsylvania, I made my commitment to God through Christ. Though I've failed Him many times, He's never failed me. And I hope to spend my entire life thanking Him by both word and behavior.

Through this part of the chapter, I have been talking about *saying* "Thanks" to those who have given us so much; but important as that is, it isn't enough. When you recognize your debt, it requires more of you than just saying "thanks"; it requires you to *give* thanks . . . to exhibit it in your life.

That's why commitment is so important. Remember my words: Commitment will drive you and motivate you to overcome laziness; commitment will not allow you to let anything interfere with the usefulness of your life and tarnish the respect you've earned; commitment will mean you'd rather fail, trying, than not try.

The Dream of a Perfect World 127

We're gone over four reasons the president in the parable failed:

1. He had a lust for laziness
2. He had a passion for popularity
3. He had a fear of failure
4. He had an incomplete commitment

In discussing each of the reasons, I've tried to show both how they contribute to failure and how they can be avoided or overcome. I know you're strong enough to overcome the negative effect of having me restate them as negatives; turn them into positives and put them to work . . . take a chance on working, not for a *perfect* world, maybe—that won't come until the Lord makes it perfect—but at the least for a *better* world. As you've been told so often, it will be in your hands; you might as well start now if you don't like the shape it's in.

Let me close with a story about *The Messiah*, Handel's magnificent oratorio on the life of Jesus Christ.

I like all music—jazz, country and western, ballets; I tolerate the classics pretty well, and I *feel* soul music; you'll think I'm a hopeless square when I tell you my favorite secular music is any song with words by Oscar Hammerstein; but when it comes to religious music, my favorites are *The Messiah* and the hymn, "When I Survey the Wondrous Cross," by Watts.

It fascinates me that one man could take the whole story of the life of our Lord and put it into such glorious music; and even if I didn't like the music, I'd stand there in awe of how much brain power Handel must have possessed.

Every year in London, as in many of our cities, there is a special performance of *The Messiah* in the famous Royal Albert Hall. The London Symphony is the orchestra. The best voices out of all the choirs in Europe are chosen for the chorus.

But it doesn't stop there, the finest voices in Europe are

the soloists. The pay is not much, as performances go, but there is the prestige. When you can add to your credits that you sang as a soloist in *The Messiah* with the London Symphony at Royal Albert Hall, your price for other concerts goes up!

Performances are Friday night, Saturday night and Sunday afternoon. Thursday morning before the first performance, people are sent down to the slums of London to give out passes to those who could not afford to come otherwise and invite them to a dress rehearsal Thursday night. The agreement with the people is this: "First, you must promise that you will clean up before you come. Second, you will arrive on time. Third, you will try to understand the music. And fourth, whether you do understand it or not, you will be quiet until the end of the performance."

For a number of years they had a small conductor, who was only 4 feet 11 inches tall. In the year I'm telling you about, on dress rehearsal night, they came and filled Royal Albert Hall—a beautiful hall with tier on tier of balconies. The orchestra filled the stage, with the chorus above and behind them; the little conductor came out, the soloists took their seats, and the dress rehearsal began.

When they came to my favorite solo, "I Know That My Redeemer Liveth," with a text from the Book of Job in the Old Testament set to the most lovely and moving melody, a beautiful young lady stood to sing it. She was as lovely as the music, and her voice matched her beauty. Everything she did seemed perfect; her posture, her breath control, her enunciation—everything showed that she had been taught well and had trained herself almost to perfection.

The audience, from the slums of London, people who weren't supposed to understand good music, was hushed in awe when she finished; you could tell they wished they could applaud.

The Dream of a Perfect World

But they were suddenly shocked as the conductor stopped everything cold. He put his baton down, climbed down from his podium, crossed to where the soprano had just sat down, and bent to say to her, "Young lady, tell me. Do you know that *your* Redeemer liveth?"

She just blushed for a moment and then said, softly, "Yes, sir. Yes, I know."

He said, "Then why don't you sing like you know?"

He went back to the podium, said something to the orchestra, raised his baton, and began again the introduction to her solo. She stood and began to sing.

Her posture was just as erect, her breath control just as exact, her enunciation just as clear and precise; she hit the high notes with just as much ease, the low notes with just as much grace; but this time, her performance had an indefinable extra. It can't be taught; it can't be bought; it can only be sought. This time she sang as though the words had been written with the blood of her heart, sang with every part of her being, "I Know That My Redeemer Liveth."

When she had finished and again sat down, you might have seen her perfect posture slump a little, because she had truly put everything she had into her singing—but the audience didn't notice. They didn't feel like applauding; they were trying to wipe away tears without being noticed. And again the conductor stopped everything to come over to the soprano. This time, he put his arm around her shoulders and said, "I'm sorry. You *do* know . . . for you have just told us so."

I'll let you choose your own moral from that story.

In talking to high schoolers all over the country, I've never said, "Go out and lead a crusade." I've never said, "Go out and wear a sign that says, 'This is what I believe.'" All I've said is that with all the talent you have, you should repay the debt you owe . . . to your parents . . . to your school . . . to America.

Whatever you do to win popularity, don't lose your self-respect or the respect of others. When there's a chance to do something, however small, even if you know you might fail, be willing to take the risk. And do these things because you know you are a debtor, as a way of saying "thanks."

Then what you are and what you believe will show forth, as it did in the young soprano soloist. Then the way you talk, the way you behave, the way you live, will all say to anyone, "Watch that one . . . there's something about him. He knows what it is to say, 'Thank you.' So he'll use what he has to the best of his ability." And no one can ask for more.

You'll be living my favorite statement of life: "I'm only one, but I am one. I cannot do everything, but I can do something." And I, for one, am simply not going to let that which I cannot do keep me from doing that which I can do.

One fairly good life is the least I can contribute—and so can you.

Prefix to Chapter V

THE SPIRIT OF '76

Without the principles expressed in the Scout Oath, Scouting would not be worth the time of any serious adult. With them it is worth the best we can give it, for our real aim in working with boys is to help shape the future of our nation and the world.

A man who believes that Scouting is worth his time, who has given generously of both his time and talent in support of Scouting, is Dr. Thomas Stephens Haggai. He is active regionally and nationally with the Boy Scouts of America, and has been honored with awards including the Silver Buffalo for distinguished service to boyhood in his role as minister, youth counsellor, radio commentator and humorist.

Dr. Haggai speaks on contemporary Scouting and laces his speeches with inspiration and motivation. His dedication to the concepts of Scouting in the future of America are well emphasized in his speech, "The Spirit of '76," which he is asked to give more than 30 times each year.

Alden Barber
Chief Scout Executive

V. The Spirit of '76

It was four-thirty in the morning, April 19, 1775—half an hour to full light. Eight hundred British soldiers and marines, under the command of Lt. Colonel Smith and Major Pitcairn, had been dispatched the night before to march to Lexington, take the revolutionaries, rabble-rousers or patriots (take your pick, depending on your point of view), Sam Adams and John Hancock, then proceed six miles farther to Concord and destroy a stock of arms that might be used by the people if trouble should break out.

His Excellency, General Thomas Gates, Governor of the Colony of Massachusetts and until recently Commander in Chief of all His Majesty's forces in North America, was determined to prevent trouble. Before he became Governor, the colonists had been permitted to form their own militia and store their own arms; that had been a mistake, but now a quiet night march by a good force of men would seize the arms and prevent an armed rebellion.

All through the night, couriers had been riding from Boston with the word that the troops had embarked in small boats and were moving—where, no one knew. Both Paul Revere and William Dawes got to Lexington before one o'clock in the morning, to warn Adams and Hancock; they had also alerted all the houses along their ways. Immediately, the bell called out the militia, but no one had seen the troops so the men were dismissed, with orders to reassemble at the sound of the drum. Some went to their homes; the rest gathered at a tavern near the green.

The British troops had landed in Cambridge, opposite Boston—and then waited until two in the morning for provisions. Then they set out for Lexington, "by wading through a very long ford up to our middles"; though they knew the countryside was stirring, they were not detected until they were a mile and a quarter from Lexington.

The drum beat, the bells rang again; and the militia, under Captain John Parker, straggled back to the green, sure this was another false alarm. They "were in a confused state, only a few of them being drawn up (in ranks) . . . There were present as spectators about forty more, scarce any of whom had arms." And the troops, with muskets loaded and primed and bayonets fixed, marched on.

Captain Parker said to his men, "Don't fire unless fired upon. But if they want a war, let it begin here." Major Pitcairn rode out in front of his troops and shouted, "Disperse, ye rebels! Lay down your arms!" The militiamen didn't disperse; someone fired a pistol; there were two musket shots, then rolls of musketry from both sides. Three colonials were killed; ten colonials and one British regular were wounded. The militia dispersed, the troops marched off to Concord.

The British found stronger resistance when they reached Concord; they did seize a small quantity of arms, but the colonials were receiving reinforcements every minute; by mid-morning the countryside was literally up in arms. Colonel Smith, sensing disaster, ordered a return to Boston. All the way back, the colonials kept up what amounted to a running ambush on the British column; by the time they were rescued by a force marching out from Boston, they had suffered more than two hundred and fifty casualties; Colonel Smith himself was wounded. Actually, that's not very accurate fire from the Americans; it has been estimated that nearly 4,000 men had shot at them all day!

The Spirit of '76

That long day, beginning before dawn, was the real start of the War of Revolution, although the Declaration of Independence was fourteen and a half months in the future. And the colonists who fought that day were typical of the men (and women) who were to carry the brunt of the war through the long years to Cornwallis' surrender at Yorktown in 1783.

They called themselves Minutemen, because they were ready to drop their work and turn soldier in a minute; and they fought because they knew no other way to achieve what they believed in. A report from one of the British officers who made the march to Concord and back tells how fervent that belief was: "The enthusiastic zeal with which those people have behaved must convince every reasonable man what a difficult and unpleasant task General Gage has before him. Even weamin had firelocks. One was seen to fire a blunder bus between her father and husband, from their windows; there they three with an infant child soon suffered the fury of the day."

"The fury of the day" was sudden death from musket or bayonet. But, believing in the rightness of their cause, the Minutemen—and their "weamin"—were willing to pay even that price. Because of them, we enjoy freedom today.

But today has its own fury, and we again need citizens who will respond to the call of duty.

This time, the call is not to fight a physical war, against an enemy who can be destroyed by firepower or exhausted on a field of battle. We must fight another kind of battle—for the minds and spirit of our youth.

Like St. Paul, we face the challenge of wrestling not against flesh and blood, but against principalities, against powers, against rulers of darkness. And the help we need is not from sociologists, behavioral scientists and other professionals in the arts and sciences of the mind; our need is for men of good character to give of their time to provide guidance and example for our youth.

The Minutemen were organized into militia companies; they knew the value of organization. We, too, must organize. The call today is for over two million adult Scouters to enlist in BOYPOWER '76, following the historic purpose of Scouting: That we have the privilege of working with boys of great promise, helping them train themselves and make the proper decisions for today and for tomorrow.

It may sound boastful for me to suggest that the Boy Scouts of America should be the place of leadership in a battle to rescue our youth from a loss of direction or, still worse, a misdirection—a purposeful attempt to lead them astray. Actually, it is not a boast, but a challenge. BOYPOWER '76 is a culmination of 62 years of effort; Boy Scouts of America is the largest organization reaching and leading young men (and now young ladies, through the Explorer program); it is only natural that we should recognize the size and scope of the problem and then marshall our forces to meet it. We could not sit idly by while America slowly comes to realize that our youth need direction and says, in consternation, "What can be done? Who will lead?"

We felt that Scouting had to take the lead, or else announce its withdrawal from the scene. That's the same thing as quitting—and we've never been quitters.

So here's the challenge of BOYPOWER '76: We're going to reach and involve a representative one-third of America's youth in Scouting by the 200th anniversary of our nation.

One-third. One out of every three. That's an assignment!

But the challenge is not in numbers alone! We're going to involve this representative one third of our nation's youth in a pragmatic program that is as meaningful to the boy in the inner city as to the boy in the suburbs; as powerful in attract-

The Spirit of '76

ing the boy in the metropolitan area as the boy in the open country; as stimulating to the rich boy as the poor boy, to the one who is black as the one who is white; and finally, this must be a program that will help each of these boys in his character development. This is our commitment.

The colonials of the 1770's heard and read patriots who issued a call to greatness for a new nation. Before 1976, we must learn again the lessons they taught; we must be restless, resourceful, ingenious in inventing new ways to instill in every American boy a sense of the value of what he has been given as a birthright. We must show that we believe in change, to meet today's problems—but that change can be achieved without first destroying our society; we will enlist boys who will help us change without battering down the structure of society.

Like 1776, this will be a revolution—but a cultural revolution, where the Minutemen of today must work in spanning the gaps between people of different creeds, colors and ages. The building of bridges across these gaps is the unfinished business our generation is bequeathing to the next; BOY-POWER '76 recognizes that future Americans must rely on the leadership we cultivate today in the lives of these boys.

How will this be done? We have committed ourselves to a program using the most sophisticated management and humanistic techniques and teachings that have yet been developed, and on principles that are ageless. The methods of the Boy Scouts of America are always up-to-date; the motivation has the experience of generations of testing and successful leadership behind it.

Let me put it this way. The Boy Scouts of America is built on three basic principles. At every meeting, whether it's at the Cub level, the Scout level or the Explorer level, each boy is led—not pushed but led—to three commitments:

1. To express his faith in his Creator
2. To express his dedication to his country
3. To express his concern for his fellowman

Think of all the things you desire for today's youth—for your own sons or daughters. Do they not all rest on these commitments? Can you think of a better package of ideals than this?

Let's look at each of them, in detail, beginning with the commitment of faith. I'm not saying the Boy Scouts of America should try to bail our churches and synagogues out of their tragic loss of attendance; this is not the organization to become involved, nationwide, in sectarian development, denominational growth, or any church's pride in its ability to add names to its rolls. No, I'm talking about an individual commitment that is instilled in every boy.

As soon as he enters Scouting, he is introduced to a program that is built on Scout law, based on the ancient Decalogue that God handed to his servant Moses on Mount Sinai.

I believe we've done our young people a disservice, in allowing them to grow up with a wrong idea about God and His laws. In fact, I have a talk I use on campuses, entitled "The Rationale of the Ten Commandments," to combat the misinterpretations I've found. Too many young people—and even many of us adults—picture God as a snoop who paces up and down, looking down at us on earth, and when He finds you doing something you really enjoy, He thinks to Himself, "That's something people like to do!" Then He slaps your wrist and says, "Naughty, naughty . . . you can't do that! You like it too much!"

I don't mean to be sacrilegious, but God is often pictured to our youth as a "kill-joy", a "party-pooper", as they would put it; so I show them, in my talk, that God didn't need the

Ten Commandments for *His* sake; they were given to man for man's survival. They are simple rules governing man's relationship with God and ordering his relationships with his fellowman.

All that Scouting teaches begins with and rests on Scout law which is, as I said, based on the ancient Decalogue. By building Scouting on the Scout law, we say to each young man who enters Scouting that ours is a society of law, that we want people to be free, and the only way freedom is possible is within law. When law is abolished, the result is not freedom—it's chaos.

The root of character is conscience, and each of us begins developing his conscience at his mother's breast; our knowledge of right and wrong, and our ability to choose between them, is taught us from our earliest days. As we grow, we may push our mother's teachings into hidden recesses of the mind, substituting other, more popular, values. But repeating the Scout law, over and over, at every meeting, brings these teachings again to the front. The words of the Law, respect for the law, call us back to the very roots of character.

But Scouting doesn't allow any lad to stop with just memorizing the law; it is easy to be able to dot the "i" and cross the "t" and not understand it. So we take each boy out into the great outdoors and help him engage in real activities so he can see how necessary and right it is for him to be trustworthy, loyal, helpful, friendly, courteous, kind, obedient, cheerful, thrifty, brave, clean and reverent. He soon learns that the Scout law helps him survive not only in the woods but on the streets. In the outdoors he sees that there are laws of nature, and he soon learns to understand that man never is able to break them, but man can be broken by the law of God.

To me, this is so basic it seems obvious; but people often see only the surface and think Scouting is only a recreation program. We only use recreation in its true meaning—to help people recreate themselves. From the very beginning, Scouting is a program of moral education, and our first principle is that a youngster must learn to express his faith in his Creator.

The second principle, that each boy in Scouting expresses his devotion to his country, is just as simple and meaningful. I'm not talking about a program where boys shout their allegiance to their country above any other; I'm not talking about the kind of program advocated by the super patriots who look for a communist under every stump and behind every program that involves change. It is of such people that Dr. Johnson said, "Patriotism is the last refuge of a scoundrel." They seek to belittle others, not make them grow; they project their own insecurity on the world and invent a faith in a nation to defend them from their own fears.

When Scouts meet, they salute the flag (as is only proper); they learn how it is to be displayed, even how it is to be folded (which is only good manners); these are only the surface of their feeling of allegiance to their country.

Scouting is a development program; each boy or girl is challenged to develop the best that's in him. But there's more to it than just the development; it's also a system which provides measurements for each person's development, and rewards for his achievements. In days gone by, we used to think of this in terms of rank; today, industry is coming to understand that the way you motivate people to do their best is to give them a sense of their own accomplishment, rather than having them always obey orders and do what they're told. Scouting knew that, years ago; each rank a boy achieves is a public recognition of his having met certain tests and achieved certain development.

Just what does this have to do with citizenship? It helps each lad dispel a dream and realize a reality.

The Spirit of '76

The dream is that we in America seem to be hung up on a Messiah complex; we seem to believe that soon some person or some group will appear with quick, easy solutions to all our problems; as soon as we find that person or that group, all our troubles are going to be done away with. Thank God, that's not the way democracy works, and Scouting teaches our youth how it really does work.

There are seldom instant answers in a democracy, and progress is often slower than we would like. But progress depends on having me put my best effort toward the solution of problems; that effort is multiplied by your best effort; and our efforts are multiplied by the efforts of all the others in the nation. Each person is called on to do his best, to be his best. And Scouting teaches every boy that he has an obligation to prepare himself and develop himself for citizenship, that the greatest contribution he can make to his country is the best of himself.

In the development program of Scouting, he progresses from basic, individual skills necessary for survival in the wild—swimming, hiking, knot-tying, and all the rest—to such exciting subjects as astrophysics, oceanography, microbiology; but with his individual interests, he also learns avenues of community service.

I don't mean to have you underestimate the importance of the individual interests; facing audiences of businessmen almost every day, somewhere in America or elsewhere around this world, I'm frequently fascinated to have men tell me that they didn't find their careers through courses in school nor even through the guidance of their parents; often, they say, working on a merit badge in Scouting uncovered latent talents they never knew they had. Just recently, a doctor in Illinois told me how his son, attending a Scout Jamboree in Valley Forge, prepared some tapes to send back to the people who had made it possible for him and his friends to attend; these tapes uncovered a real radio talent; and the boy, now grown, is started on a very successful career in broadcasting.

When we say that Scouting is built on citizenship, it's built on the development of each person's best, and the giving of that best to the country and to the community in which he lives. This dedication to develop the best that's in us and use it for the betterment of our neighborhoods and our nation acts like leaven in the lump of indecision and misdirection that our contemporary society seems to be.

The third commitment each Cub, Scout and Explorer makes, to express his concern for his fellow man, involves a serious subject that has caused more jokes about Scouting than any other aspect of our program—the daily good deed. But it is serious.

A couple of years ago, when I was in my native state of Michigan to address a Chamber of Commerce banquet, I was driving with my cousin, John, who lives there, and he asked me about my caring for people. He said, "Tom, I can't understand it. We were raised pretty much the same way, even with the difference in our ages, and I love my wife and son, and when I have time left over, I care about other people. But you *always* care about other people. What gave you this concern? How come you're so constantly involved in helping people?"

My answer may have surprised him, and it may surprise you; but it's true. I said, "It may sound corny, Johnny, but when I was a lad, I was an active Boy Scout and while I was still in a very formative period, that put into the warp and woof of my fiber that I was not to live a single day, not one 24-hour period, without doing something for someone else, whether it was something that was expected of me, something I was called on to do, or something that was my idea. And the teaching stuck. I cannot rest comfortably at the end of a day unless I have done something for someone else."

The Spirit of '76

At the close of my last speaking year, a reporter asked me what I had learned about America during the course of the year. I said that it had been brought home to me, again and again, that America is two hundred million plus people who are lonely, frustrated, scared. In our society of lonely people, a good deed often rekindles some lost faith in our country and in living.

Scouting's emphasis on a good deed a day requires that at least once a day, each of us has to think about something outside the shell of our lives. In some ways, our youth have put their elders to shame, by showing us how, even though each of us can do only a little, a lot of us put together can get a lot done.

Think how we have translated this into one big good deed with the introduction of Scouting's project SOAR—Save Our American Resources. While lots of people were just talking about ecology (and I often think if we could get the ecology freaks to hush a bit, we could clean up our atmosphere!), our young people went out, all over this country, and actually put good ecology into practice. I remember a Boy Scout Council—and not too large a Council, at that, on the West Coast—that picked up 76 tons of debris in one day! Our Scouts have cleaned up river banks; they've helped move unauthorized junkyards; they've cleaned up vacant lots and picnic areas . . . they've cleaned up after us, and they've eloquently brought home to us that we must stop strangling ourselves with our discarded filth.

I mean to take nothing from Project SOAR, but more recently scouting has undertaken a new project that is (and I say this carefully, not wanting to be guilty of overstatement) the most exciting application of a segment of our society working to correct a social ill that, in my brief lifetime, I have witnessed.

If I were to ask you, "What is the biggest problem facing our youth today?", I am sure you would answer, "Drugs."

That is where Scouting has pitched its newest tent, as we introduce a program called OPERATION REACH.

When we talk about the problem of drugs and drug abuse, we must want to be more than superficial with our answers; we must dig. It has been my pleasure to work with many groups, including many in military life; with all of them, I have explored their answers to the question, "Why drugs?" Many, many explanations are advanced; but the one reason that is given more frequently than all the others put together, is that when a young person feels alone, misunderstood, put down, not accepted, then he turns to drugs. Whether he tries marijuana or one of the other, more extreme forms, the common ingredient they offer the user is that, through their use, he is now in a world of security. He feels self-sufficient; drugs provide him an avenue of escape into another world—a world he thinks will be better than the world he has either rejected or that he feels has rejected him.

Am I overstating the case? A study recently completed, with money from the Rockefeller Fund, found that about 40 per cent of our young people, in America today, do not believe they have a real friend whom they can trust, or to whom they can turn in trouble.

40 per cent? I may not be very bright in math, but that means 40 out of every 100 kids in *my* town, 2 out of every 5 that I find on the street corner, do not believe they have a single friend they can trust.

That is the most poignant evidence that they are suffering from more than just a generation gap; they even feel cut off from each other. And with such aloneness, and such a feeling of rejection, the promise of drugs offers a natural escape. The drug world is painted as being beautiful, sweet. The pusher promises you no more pain; everything's coming up roses; in fact, the pusher is the one who promises you a rose garden, to paraphrase the pop song.

I can still hear the voice of a brilliant young airman, in

The Spirit of '76

England telling me that the only friends he had, the only ones he could trust, were his fellow users.

All right, the drug problem is real. The next question is, "What can we do, and how do we do it?" A great guy like Art Linkletter has literally spent himself talking about drug abuse, especially since the loss of his lovely daughter, Diane. He really stirs us up. But there's one problem: He's talking to us, he's stirring *us* up; he isn't talking to the young drug pushers and victims. They wouldn't listen to him if he tried talking to them.

I'm asked to talk on this subject, quite often, and I do the best I can; and people sometimes respond with a great deal of enthusiasm. But it's *my* crowd responding; and I'm ten years beyond the "trustable" age of 30.

Our problem is that we are talking about the drug problem to each other, as adults; and the only sound way to correct the problem is on a peer level—youth talking to youth.

But before I quit talking to you as an adult, let me add one other proviso: It is important for us to think in terms of preventive medicine. All of us are sympathetic with any person who is hooked and hooked hard; but if he is on hard drugs, then the only help for him must come from the medical men and the psychiatrists in the institutions that deal with hard drug users. It's too late for any concerned, well-meaning but untrained lay person to reach and help him.

What Scouting wants to do is stop where we are and prevent any further growth of drug abuse; and this is the thrust of OPERATION REACH.

Here are the five basic principles of OPERATION REACH:

> REACH   for the real "highs" instead of going for a poor substitute like drugs.
> REACH   for real friends—and stand by them.
> REACH   for warm and open relations with my

> parents, other members of my family, and my friends.
>
> REACH an understanding with myself by taking an open stand against drugs.
>
> REACH others by telling them about OPERATION REACH.

They sound simple, don't they? Do you want to say, "They seem *too* simple?" No, one of our problems is that we have made the whole thing too complicated.

This is a program which identifies resources young people can turn to, instead of a program that submerges them in a sea of concern. Resources are the things you can use to act; concern is just worrying a great deal. We have complicated the drug situation with a lot of useless worry rather than turning to our resources.

But this must be a kid-to-kid program; our role as adults is to provide a bridge between the long past, that has proved the tragedy of what drugs do, and the new future in which young people will be kept from their abuse.

Can it work? It has, and it will. Scouting did not go into OPERATION REACH blindly; four cities—Philadelphia, Los Angeles, Providence and Des Moines—tried it as a pilot program for several months. Only after startling and remarkable results—finding that young people have the capacity to empathize, watching the realization dawn on them that they were really reaching out and it was working—only then did we make it a national program.

Even though OPERATION REACH is a positive program, designed to keep young people from ever getting started with drugs, Scouting is also a resource for any young person who may have gotten started, been busted, and now wants a new direction in his life. Historically, we are both conditioned and structured to give a sense of belonging. Scouting has always been made up of small units, whether it be the den of Cubbing, the patrol of Scouting, or the committee of Exploring. Every person who has a part in any of these units is given a certain responsibility. But don't forget that with that responsibility, the unit also gives a sense of belonging. Our units have a camaraderie of fellowship; they foster a fraternal feeling. They have been, and can be, lifesaving stations on the road back.

Now, even if you understood it in the beginning, you see more clearly what I mean when I say that the Boy Scouts of America, using the most effective means possible, is projecting eternal principles which go back to the basic laws of God. In Scouting, a young man is led to affirm his faith, pledge his allegiance, and commit himself in service to his fellowman.

My comfort and my confidence come from my knowledge that our principles are sound and they will, therefore, succeed. I can help our projects succeed, but the whole program will succeed even without me, because even if our principles were again put on the scaffold, they would rise again and live forever.

This, then, is what Scouting can do to provide direction and example for our young people; these are the principles and the programs with which Scouting is taking the lead in fighting the battle for the minds of our youth. What does this program ask of us adults? What commitments must the modern Minutemen make?

The answer is neither dramatic nor melodramatic; just two things are necessary.

First, you must be concerned.

I know; your immediate reaction is that you *are* concerned. If you weren't, why would you be reading this written version of one of my talks?

I wish I could say that anything that superficial proves your concern.

My awakening came as a minister. I found that, many

times, those who spoke the most about young people, those who expressed, verbally, the greatest concern, really were not concerned at all when you scratched beneath the surface. Some talked about today's young people as a cover-up for their own "Roaring 20's." Others talked about today's young people because they felt a sense of guilt and failure about their raising of their own children. Still others talked about the sins of today's youth and gained a sensual thrill as they went through detail after detail, recounting the practices of our extreme young people with the same mouth-watering delight that they might whisper about some orgy that was supposed to have taken place in their community. Then, of course, there are also those who talked about young people because that's just as good a topic of conversation as motherhood and babies.

Here's how I found out, to my surprise, that there's a difference between expressing concern and feeling it. Early one morning the custodian of our church asked me to come with him, quickly, over to the church building. As we went in the side door of the education building, I realized why he was so upset. Everywhere, disarray. Chairs broken to pieces, and the pieces had been used to scratch and mar the walls; I began to figure the cost of new plaster. Windows had been broken; my mental estimate of damages mounted. Paint streaks had been straggled down the walls of halls. Toys had been torn apart in the nursery. Hymn books had been stomped upon in the sanctuary.

As I looked at the wreckage, my temper got the best of me. I turned to our custodian, whose name was also Tom, and said, "Start trying to repair what you can, while I call the authorities. Then we'll try to appraise the actual damage." Really, I wanted to get him out of my sight so I could blow my top. I wasn't filled with "righteous indignation"; I was just plain mad, trying to figure what kind of homes could produce youth who, with complete lack of respect, could do this kind of thing to a house of worship.

As I walked back through the building, I saw something I hadn't noticed before. Maybe my rage had blinded me, but in every classroom, in every assembly room, and down every corridor I saw, pointing toward me, a human finger. Oh, not literally—and yet I think I saw that finger pointing toward me more clearly than if it had been flesh and blood. And I heard a voice saying, "Get mad if you want! Blow your stack if it'll make you feel better. Go ahead and blame the kids who could do this kind of wanton damage—but you might do well to examine your own heart at the same time. You are the minister, the heart of your congregation; you believe the church should be the heart of the community. What have *you* done to teach the young people of the area anything better than this?"

I went back to my study in the parsonage a greatly rebuked young man. There I buried my head in my arms and asked God to forgive me. Then I sat up and did what should have been done long before—I called the local office of the Boy Scouts.

We organized a Scouting program to provide the character development and leadership training that had been missing, and I began my romance with Scouting as a pastor. My experience was not what someone *said* Scouting could do, it was firsthand; I *saw* what Scouting could do to give purpose and direction to our young people.

This experience also taught me the difference between superficial and genuine concern. Because Scouting was adopted as a church program, it was included in the church budget. Budget time is always a good indicator of the health of a church. We would go right through our mission program without a question; right through salaries without a question (and that really should have made me suspicious!). Then we would come to activities; listed right at the top of the youth program was "Boy Scouts of America"—all three units.

Then a man in the back of the room would begin clearing his throat; finally, he would stand up, very pompously, roll his eyes toward Heaven—not because he was spiritual but because he didn't have the courage to look me in the eye while he said what he had to say—and this is about what he had to say: "Now, Pastor, I don't know if the money given by the good people of the Lord"—that's a phrase that always turns me off; I've always wondered what right we had to say we're good people of the Lord . . . let the Lord say that and I'll believe it—"I don't know if the money given by the good people of the Lord should be used for something as secular as the Boy Scouts of America." Let me interrupt him again; how could it be said that a program based on affirmation of faith, loyalty to country and service to fellowman was not the proper business of the church? Anyway, he would conclude, "I would like to have us restudy this portion of the budget and table this particular item for the moment."

Well, when something is "tabled" in the Baptist church it means that it is gone—it will never be brought up again. And I had to sweat blood to get these people to do what they said they wanted to do—have a program that could enlist, encourage, and guide our young people.

That's how I learned the difference between superficial and genuine concern. Of course, I feel every church should have Scouting. Otherwise, who do you blame your broken windows on? If your troop was camping out, 30 miles away, and a window got broken, some of our church committee members figured they hiked in during the night, broke the window, and hiked back to camp!

I'm reminded of a story; I can't vouch for the facts, but

The Spirit of '76

the story is true in spirit, at least. A lady who had been constantly criticizing the Scouting program of her church ran up to her pastor excitedly. "Pastor, Pastor," she said, "now Scouting just has to go!"

"Well, sister," the pastor said, "you've been saying that for some time. Why this time?"

"I just walked into the sanctuary and looked up to our baptismal pool just in time, Pastor, to see a naked Boy Scout climbing out. He'd been *swimming!*"

I have to add, for you non-Baptists, that where you just dry clean new members, we make sure they're clean all over.

Anyway, the pastor paused for a moment, and then said, "My dear, if he was dressed as you suggest, I can see how you could tell he was a boy—but how could you tell he was a Boy Scout?"

That lady was concerned *about* Scouting; I am asking you to be concerned *with* Scouting, and to demonstrate your concern rather than just talking about it.

Concern means doing something. If you have a committee assignment, show up for the committee meetings, with your assignment completed. If you are an institutional representative, make sure the institution you represent really supports Scouting. Try to build the proper attitude; Scouting isn't something you brag on as an "image-builder" for your church, your company, your civic club or your union; it's a way your organization can contribute a real service to your community and your country.

Scouting doesn't need the support of "good names," or support in name only. It is not benefited when you or I "lend our names"; *we* are benefited by being part of Scouting!

My feeling about the adults in Scouting proving their concern is so serious that I'm probably the only person who speaks all over the country trying to get adults out of Scouting. What I say is simple: If you are not going to take seriously whatever your responsibility is, then Scouting will benefit with your resignation. And there are a lot of adult Scouters who ought to get out.

I've seen a Court of Honor where neither parents nor some Scout officials showed up—and the motivation of the boys damaged beyond repair. I've seen Scout masters resign, and everybody wonder why, never questioning the fact that the Troop Committee had not met for a solid year!

Actually, when I think back on incidents like these I've seen or heard about, there have not been very many adult Scouters who have shirked their responsibilities this way. But the way I feel, one is too many! So if you're on a district committee, be there! If you're on a council committee, you weren't given the post as an honor, but to work at it, so work at it!

Each year I give about eighty talks at various Scout activities and banquets, and I don't thank people too often for their work in Scouting. My feeling about volunteer work—and you and I are volunteers, even if there was some arm-twisting involved—is that if we don't give the same commitment and dedication to work we've volunteered for as we give our livelihood, we are being basically dishonest—and I certainly would not think you to be that. But if we do that which we are paid to do more conscientiously than that which we volunteer to do, that means our virtues are for sale, and I wouldn't want that said about either you or me.

So let me sum up the first commitment Scouting asks of today's Minutemen with a series of questions; I suggest we examine ourselves thus: "Do we believe in this program of Scouting? Are we genuinely concerned that it does all it can do for youth? Are we willing to make our concern and Scouting's concern merge?"

Scouting needs all of us who can honestly answer "Yes!" to those questions; it has no need for any who have any doubts about the answers.

All right, Scouting asks first for your concern, and second, yes, it asks for your contribution.

You've probably been waiting for me to get to that point, knowing my background as a Baptist minister. And I have to admit that it troubles me, speaking to as many as a thousand people at a Scouting function, not to be allowed to take up an offering! It's not just my Baptist background; on top of that, I'm descended from the Lebanese tradition. The Lebanese are descendants of the Phoenicians, the master-pirates of the eastern Mediterranean in ancient times; the basic definition of us now is that we have the ability to buy from a Jew and sell to a Scot—and make a profit on the deal!

When I talk about contribution, one important reason you may not have considered is that it is the second leg in getting young people to believe in our sincerity. We can *say* all we want to about being concerned about them, but they just don't believe us until they see our concern in our commitment of time and in our commitments of contributions.

I haven't a single reservation about promoting giving to Scouting because, obviously, I believe in the cause it serves, but also because I've never seen an organization so thorough and demanding in accounting for its funds. Whether it's a Cub pack, a Scout troop, a council or a region, you can ask at any moment and find out exactly what your money is doing.

For many years, Scouting didn't talk very much about money; how come now it's asking? For a couple of very good reasons.

First, when I was a lad, and even up until quite recently, we could say that every boy wanted to be a Scout. That's not true today.

When you consider that we have the lowest attendance in proportion to church membership we have ever recorded, when you consider there's not a single civic club whose membership is growing as fast as our population, when you consider that fraternities and sororities on our campuses are being pushed to try to keep their membership filled, you begin to realize that joining is just not the "in" thing in America today. And Scouting is feeling it; we can no longer say that if we can get the leadership for a Scout troop, there will be plenty of boys to join it.

Today we must have more than good organization; we have to go out and enlist the boys. This takes promotion, public relations, even advertising. You say, "Well, isn't that all contributed?" Yes, a great deal is contributed to Scouting; it is one of the continuing projects of the Advertising Council, which prepares and coordinates annual advertising and public relations programs; and newspaper, magazines, radio and television are generous in their contribution of public service space and time for our messages. But as the effort becomes more important, it also requires money; we have to have materials that reach out and grab the attention, and we have to pay for their preparation, whether in printed form or commercials.

So we now need more money than we did for promotion; we also need more money for salaries.

I am constantly amazed at the high caliber of men we get in Scouting. We require professional training of them; they should, in all fairness, be able to require professional salaries of us. To keep our best men, we must be able to pay them at least approximately as much as they could command in some other field.

I learned something about this as a pastor. Although I never discussed salary with any church I served, I know I was able to do a more effective job because my churches were always generous with me.

It used to be that church budget committees had the idea that if you keep a man low-salaried, you keep him humble—and praying. (That's for sure!) When I didn't have much income, I was really praying; but not for anyone else—I was praying for my own needs! But when I was taken care of comfortably, then I could spend my energy fulfilling my real role in life—caring for others. The same thing is true of the professionals in Scouting, whether you're talking about a young fireball or a tried and true executive. He should not have to worry about money, but should have the social standing his office requires; and whether we like it or not, his social standing is pretty well determined by how much money he takes home. Ours is a materialistic society, and a man who cannot be on the same social level with the people he is to lead is terribly handicapped.

Another reason we're talking about money now is that we need more manpower, particularly for the Explorer program. Probably fewer than 10 per cent of our councils now have adequate professional help for Exploring. It's a highly specialized job; we know that, difficult as it may be to work with Scouts, it is even more difficult to work with older teenagers. We have to have more trained professionals for the Exploring program; it also costs more than the other levels of Scouting in unexpected ways. For instance, since Explorers graduate, move out of town, go to college and in other ways are much more mobile than younger Scouts, the career survey has to be done every year; it has to be checked, worked out, then put into the hands of the right volunteers—and that all costs money.

Our money needs are not insurmountable; new sources have joined our traditional source, the individual giver. Corporations are realizing that they have to measure their giving against the needs, first, but also against what they receive; many are now giving generously to Scouting because they recognize how much they receive in return.

Bequests are another important source, and I'd like to suggest that many people, even of moderate means, need to reevaluate their wills and be sure Scouting is included. If my will were probated at this stage in my life, Scouting would probably just get a share of my debts—but it's in there, anyway. If you believe as I do in the importance of Scouting, it should be in yours, too.

At the same time, we can continue our direct gifts to Scouting. Don't misunderstand me; I'm grateful for the United Funds all across the country, and the money they channel to Scouting. From the time I started earning a regular income, I've given between one and two per cent of my income to the United Appeal, the Community Chest, or whatever it was called wherever I've lived. I believe in this kind of giving, but I am thankful that the United Funds are not structured so they try to take care of the total needs of any of the agencies they support. Each agency is required to raise a substantial portion of its income on its own, and this allows me the privilege of giving to a cause like Scouting which is special, and close to my heart.

But when I evaluated what I wanted to do and realized I was raising a family and couldn't expect to have a lot of surplus money, I made an insurance policy payable to Scouting. I wouldn't recommend this for everyone. Suppose my council hits a period of financial troubles; reckon how they're going to pray for my health on the next flight I take! I only mention this method to show how strongly I believe each of us must do what he can.

I have been immeasurably fortunate, though, because God gave me the idea for Tom Haggai and Associates Foundation. A group of businessmen from all over America shares with me in this foundation, under the trusteeship of a bank in High Point, N.C.; it doesn't take much each year from each man, or even from me. But when we put all our contributions together, we have a sizeable amount of money which we give, as scholarships, to young men who are dedicating their lives to professional Scouting.

Even in mentioning THA Foundation, I may have done you a disservice. Whenever someone makes a major gift, it gets publicity—as it should. That may leave the impression that the big gifts are more important than they really are. The real financial foundation for Scouting is individual contributions, whether they be small, medium-sized or large. Every one of us can give something; there's hardly an adult in any audience I address who couldn't give a dollar or two dollars a week. When you add up even that small a contribution from each person who's involved in Scouting and in our pack, troop and committee activities, we'd soon have the full amount of funding we need—without those big chunks of money that get all the publicity!

Scouting needs your contribution, because Scouting needs more funds. Look at it as an investment, not as a gift to charity. Give us an additional Scout professional and he can serve 300 volunteer Scouters and as many as 1,000 boys. In disadvantaged areas, he can serve 160 volunteers and 650 boys. For every executive we can add, we can be assured of reaching at least 1,000 more boys in most areas, at least 650 boys in even the most disadvantaged area—within a three-year period!

You can't tell me of anything that can conserve better than that investment! I'm respected as a conservative in economic policy, and I often receive letters asking me to contribute to one conservative cause or another; I always write back saying that I'm a member of the greatest program of conservation we have in the United States, called the Boy Scouts of America. I know where and how Scouting invests my dollars; I can see the tangible results, I know the boys are being reached.

So there you have the whole story of the need for Minutemen for today. We have a program that is in the process of giving a representative one third of America's youth leadership, motivation in the affirmation of their faith, commitment to their country, and devotion to service to their fellowmen. You know what is needed; we must have adults who will be a living bridge between our long past and the future, sharing in the challenges and the rewards of BOY-POWER '76. We must shake off our lethargy and be the Minutemen of our own century, not waging and winning a war against tyranny but winning crucial battles for meaning in the lives of today's youth.

Although I've said that I seldom thank people for their concern and contributions to Scouting, let me not leave you with the impression that it is a thankless task I'm recruiting you for. Let me make the point with another story.

Some time ago I happened to be in Southern California for an address at the same time my preacher brother, John, was involved in a United Church Crusade in San Diego; my address was at noon, so I could slip down and hear John that night. I was delighted, for he always inspires me.

After his sermon, when I was walking out to meet him for a late dinner, I came face to face with a man I recognized. He froze, and I froze; and he said, "You don't know who I am."

Believe me, since I meet an average of five hundred new people every night of the year, I despise having anyone say that to me. My immediate reaction was to reply, "No; if you don't know who you are, then I don't know who you are, either. Do you think I want to be smarter than you?" But this man wasn't teasing; it was just his way of starting a conversation, and he didn't deserve that kind of answer.

No, I didn't answer that way; I looked at him and said, "You'd better believe I know you; if I wouldn't embarrass you, I'd even bow to you with the same respect I've reserved for my dear friend Cardinal Cody, Archbishop of Chicago. You're Harold Anderson!"

You've never heard or read about Harold Anderson; he

never made the front page of any paper nor was he ever mentioned in any magazine. When I knew him best, he usually worked at two jobs. To my knowledge, he never lived in a new home; at this time he was living in a trailer to be near his children in Southern California. I suspect he never bought a new car right out of a showroom.

I recognized him, all right, though his hair had been a little darker when I'd last seen him, and maybe he'd stood a little bit taller; but he still wore the same prominent horn-rimmed glasses; and he was still Harold Anderson, who is worthy of life-long respect.

When my father's church organized a Scouting program, Harold Anderson was the man Dad chose to be our first Scoutmaster.

Back then, it was a good thing he didn't have a new car because we usually tore up the back seat with our piling in and out so much. Much of the extra work he did, I think, was to pay what it cost him to be our Scoutmaster. And he was the one who put it all together for me. I was raised in a tremendous home, educated in effective schools, and I grew up in a church and was taught biblical faith; Harold Anderson gave me the practical, pragmatic experience of putting all this together in living; he taught me much about sharing and serving.

That was years ago, but I never forgot his teaching or the man himself. And I went on to tell him this. "Mr. Anderson, by the grace of God I shall one day have the privilege of being in His presence. I am not humble; I have never been humble; but I shall be lucky to be on the outskirts of the crowd of people who surround God. Those places of prominence are not for me; they have to go to people like you.

"I've received my plaudits; I've enjoyed the thrill of having people actually jump up and give me standing ovations. I've received gracious kindness and generous hospitality from people around the world; I've been given more than I ever dreamed possible.

"But you, sir, are one of the people whose only praise came haltingly from the boys in your troop—boys whose lives you helped change, boys who all their lives use what they learned with and from you. Your nation and your community didn't thank you for what you did . . . they didn't know your name. You are what makes the American life good, and yet you are never known. But believe me, sir, I know you; and I've tried to express my thanks for the help you gave so generously by being of some help to others. Let me speak for all the other boys in the troop and say, 'Thank you and God bless you!'"

You have never heard of Harold Anderson; he gave part of his life in service to his fellowman and his country. You have probably never heard of John Jack either; he was one of those killed by the musket fire in the early dawn of April 19, 1775, one of the first Minutemen to die in our Revolution. You may never be known outside your own town—or perhaps even in it—for your part as a Minuteman of today.

But in choosing to help, you have chosen to invest your life, in time and in substance, in the lives of youth; you may never receive thanks here, but you are part of a crusade that I'm just square enough to believe in. I have faith that this crusade can save a nation on which many people have already given up.

The program is called the Boy Scouts of America. The crusade will succeed if we can find enough Minutemen who, in the Spirit of '76—I mean 1976—will give of themselves enough to give the program of Scouting to today's youth.